THIS BOOK

WRITTEN FROM MY HEART

IS DEDICATED TO MY MOTHER

WHO HAS ALWAYS BEEN BEHIND ME

SUPPORTING ME IN EVERY ENDEAVOR

TELLING ME I CAN BE AND DO ANYTHING

I CHOOSE.

IT IS ALSO DEDICATED TO MY TWO SONS

SCOTT AND DEREK

MY SPECIAL BLESSINGS

TABLE OF CONTENTS

TABLE OF CONTENTS

PREFACE

Since I was a child, I have always perceived myself as a healer, a caregiver, a protector of hearts. It would pain me to see the sufferings of others, from fallen butterflies to neglected animals to kids being bullied in school, and to witness those struggling to maintain life's everyday necessities, such as food, water, and shelter. I have had difficulty watching the hunted falling prey to the hunter. The worst atrocity of them all is witnessing man inflicting pain and ill will on his fellow man, which has taken place since the beginning of time. This is, and has always been, preventable. I wanted to reach out, repair others' wounds, and comfort their ailing hearts. I suppose that is why I was drawn to become an open heart surgical nurse. After working in this profession for over twenty-five years, I have had the dramatic experience of holding a beating heart in my hand. I have offered comfort and held the hands of my patients while I was wheeling them back to the operating room. Most were victims of their own abuse and neglect. I've seen in their eyes the look of not knowing, of wondering if they would wake up to see their loved ones again. I have witnessed those that never did wake up. I have spoken to families, letting them know that everything was fine and the surgery was going well, only to find out things had taken a turn for the worse when I returned to the operating room. I have spoken to families when the outcome of the surgery wasn't going so well. I have observed the frightened looks on their faces, conveying their worst fears that losing their loved one was close to becoming a reality. I have witnessed their expressions displaying their grief, loss, and despair. I have held their hands, offering comfort and hope. Yes, hope is something I encouraged in my patients' families, even when things looked hopeless, sometimes to find that things had taken a turn for the better when I returned to the surgical suite. Life and death are realities we all must face, but if we can learn to live our lives with open hearts, we can close our eyes with our last breath knowing we lived our lives in richness.

It was twenty years ago when the first notion of writing this book crept into my mind. I didn't really know what I was going to write about at the time, but I knew I had something to say. I wanted to be able to touch the lives of many, encouraging open hearts and offering guidance towards making their lives a little easier. It was five years ago that I woke up one morning and said to myself, "I am going to write a book, and it will be called *Your Life, Your Choice*." I scribbled this title down on a little piece of paper and put it in the dresser drawer beside me. Over the next few years, thoughts for this book started percolating in my head. I began to understand that everything we have and do in our lives was formed through our thoughts, choices, and actions.

I was in the midst of an unstable relationship at the time, so most of my attention went to trying to hold this partnership together. I soon realized I had to "let go" of another man who I thought I loved deeply. I was very scared and embarrassed because I had so many failed relationships in my past. Change and fear of the unknown are always frightening, but if we dare to act on our internal instincts, life always has a way of giving back to us more than we could have ever imagined. I held in my mind, with courage and strong conviction, that an abundant life was waiting for me. It was trust, belief, and continuous determination that propelled me forward. The book *Open Heart: Your Life, Your Choice* was beginning to take form.

After the breakup of this relationship I took about a year away from my many life activities other than going to work and going to the gym. Exercise, for me, was and is more than just a way to stay in shape. My aerobic time has always been a time for me to reflect and connect. Besides work and the gym, I continued upholding the bare necessities of my everyday responsibilities. I spent a lot of time alone, healing and doing inner cleansing. I knew that if I wanted to make some necessary changes in my life and put a stop to repeating the old, unhealthy patterns I was attracting, I had to take a time-out. I did a lot of meditation and connecting to my inner soul. I remodeled my home as well as cleaned and remodeled my personal being. It was through seeking my own light and inner spirit that I found my own pure self-love and abundance.

I wrote this book through love and inspiration to offer those that seek it a pathway towards their own open heart. My words come to you as a friend, showing my vulnerability and humanness. I am not a doctor, PhD, or trained counselor. I am simply a fellow human, traveling through a similar space and time, sharing this planet with you. My written words are those that come through my own life experiences. I in no way claim to have all the answers to life's mysteries or the key to unlock continuous happiness, but through this book I offer simple suggestions to create more peace, balance, and harmony within your life and others.

My experience as an open heart surgical nurse and a certified personal trainer provides me with a platform to share my professional expertise with you on how to promote health and fitness in all areas of your life. Though I am a nurse, my emphasis is on wellness rather than illness. By the end of this book, you will have increased your knowledge and understanding of how to integrate your spiritual, emotional, and physical beings into a complete, whole, and healthy package. It is my hope that you will find what

I have found, daily doses of love, peace, inner harmony, and abundance. Abundance can come in many forms, but you will see through reading this book that the key to eternal abundance is the free gift of self-love.

At times I write with warmth and understanding, and other times I write with an in-your-face attitude to push you further towards your own inner healing. As you read this book, it is my wish that you receive my words as if we were sharing a cup of coffee together. I understand what it's like to feel emotional pain and walk in unfriendly territory. Many times, when I needed a helping hand, I couldn't find one. In writing this book, I extend my hand to you and offer you support and understanding, and, when needed, a soothing blanket of comfort and hope. I want to share with you that we all have the power to create our lives exactly as we choose. Yes, we have at our disposal the power to have the life we have always dreamed of. I believe in dreaming big and never giving up. It is because of this that you are holding this book in your hands right now. If this little book has found its way to you, just know there is information in the pages to come that was meant just for you. As you begin, I ask that you read with an Open Heart. With an Open Heart, true healing, growth, and enlightenment can begin. It is Your Life and Your Choice.

YOUR LIFE, YOUR CHOICE

The Book

When we were born into this world, we came with free will and free choice. Our choices began as early as our thoughts began, and we started to create our world by the way we reacted to it. Most of us learned how to get our needs met early on. As time went on, our thoughts began to evolve, and thus the creation of our life situations started forming. We began creating our self-identity and the environment around us. As we got older, we learned that how we acted and reacted to situations from our past formed the reality of our present and our future. This book is about how we create our lives through our thoughts, choices, and actions, and how we have the power to make positive changes, if that is what we desire. A recurring theme that you will find in the pages that follow is that continuous peace is available in endless amounts to all that seek it. When you open your heart to receive the free gift of self-love, you will begin your journey towards your own self-abundance. When you learn to truly love yourself unconditionally, continuous peace and harmony can't help but flow within you and around you. Take a firm grasp of my hand and I will guide you there. At times, what you are about to read may sound harsh, but as you push through your own fears, self-doubts, and insecurities, you will find your place through self-confidence, determination, and a newfound belief in yourself. Hold steady, here we go.

As you look at your life right now, I would like you to do a personal self-inventory. Are you happy with who you are? Are you satisfied with what you have created in your personal environment and all that you have around you? Mostly it is only you who has put yourself in whatever situation you are in. Look at the people in your life. Examine your relationships, your living situation, and your job. You have created it all. Take time right now to ask yourself these simple but life-exposing questions.

- Are you generally happy?
- Are you generally sad?
- Do you feel free or do you feel trapped?
- Are you content or are you stressed?
- Do you live with joy and love or do you live with sadness and fear?
- Are you holding on to pain from the past, or have you taken time to let go, heal, and move forward?
- Are you in a healthy, harmonious relationship, or are you in a relationship that is full of turmoil, regret, and sadness?
- Is your life in balance, or are you living from one dramatic episode to another?
- Do you hold resentment or do you have forgiveness?
- Do you live with trust, or do you live in fear that somehow those around you will do you harm?
- How is your self-image?
- Do you like what you see when you look in the mirror?
- Do you feel healthy and fit, or do you live as a victim of illness?
- Do you have dreams and goals that you are striving for, or do you just live day to day, allowing whatever shows up to form your life?
- Do you appreciate all that you have around you, or do you take your positive circumstances for granted?

- Do you give back to those less fortunate, or do you hold on to your possessions tightly and believe in scarcity?
- Do you have self-love?

These are thought-provoking questions many would choose to avoid. Hopefully I have opened an inner awareness in you that encourages you to think about your current life situations. I also want you to take responsibility for everything that you have and are. It is this ownership of your life that gives you the power to make the changes you want. Because you have created it all, it is you, and only you, that can make the decision to bring forth positive change in your life. This is very important for you to grasp, because it determines whether or not you believe in yourself, whether you believe in your dreams, and whether you believe that you deserve an abundant life full of love and happiness.

You are the master of your own destiny. Every minute of every day, what comes to you is what you have put together through your thoughts, choices, and actions. Because you are now taking responsibility for it all, you can no longer blame or attribute your life situation on anyone but yourself. There are no reasons for you to stay stuck or unhappy anymore. You can now choose to think about your life situation in a positive way, with appreciation, or you can choose to see things in a negative way and focus on what is lacking, or what you do not have. Either way you will create your reality from these thoughts and emotions.

If the above thought-provoking questions caused you to squirm through identification of unwanted answers, I am here to provide you hope and show that you can change those answers to those which feel more positive. There is a way out. I am living proof, as I have suffered through many wrong choices in my life, and I found my way out. I learned to forge through adversity and never give up on my dreams.

I kept moving towards the light. I will explain what this means later. I want to share with you how I found light in darkness and how I now choose happiness over sorrow. In sharing my story, you will read about the times when I hyperventilated and didn't think I could breath, when I was on the floor and I didn't think I could get up, and the many times that I didn't think I could go on.

I know what it's like to live in fear. I had a fear of being alone and of not being loved. Fear leads to poor choices. I had to eventually learn to love myself and spend a lot of my time alone. I have finally come to a place where being alone is very comfortable. I found that my alone time was a time to remember who I was. It was in my alone time that I found my way home.

This is my journey. May all who enter into it with me find great comfort that there is a way out of emotional pain. There is always a way out, and it is our choice to find it. The light, which represents all that is good and safe, is always there. It is your choice to turn your gaze toward it. Once you fixate on it and accept it into your life you can no longer look away. If you stray, you will miss the peace and love you feel from being connected to the light, and you can't help but turn back. You will be repelled by darkness and fear. You will learn how to embrace self-love and come to realize that love is always with you. As you read and share my story, it is my hope to empower you to choose from strength and self-love rather than fear. I hope and pray that you too choose to open your heart and find your road to abundance. It is there for all of us. I invite you to now sit back, relax, and enter into this journey with me, as I describe through the next chapter my story and my path home, "Out of Darkness into Light."

MY STORY

Out of Darkness into Light

**Sometimes, in order to find yourself,
you must first lose yourself.**

I ended my first marriage of fourteen years by seeking love elsewhere. My first husband was a good man and he loved me very much. He was very affectionate and showed his love for me every day. However, for some reason I felt unful-filled. I was searching for something bigger than what I had and didn't realize I was about to open Pandora's box on love. I was a nurse working in open heart surgery at the time. The operating room can be a dangerous place for a young, attractive female, even if she is married. Temptations are everywhere with doctor/nurse interactions. Because of my profession, I spent a lot of time at work, on call, and working overtime. One of the surgeons was giving me a lot of attention, and I enjoyed it. I continued to feel unfulfilled at home and actually told my husband I was getting a lot of attention at work and that our marriage was in trouble. He ignored my warnings. Soon an advance was made by the surgeon to meet outside of the hospital. I conceded. After that meeting, my life, as I knew it, would be changed forever. The affair lasted about eighteen months, but our spouses found out three months into it. I experienced more drama through this than I have ever experienced in my life. Many lives were hurt and destroyed, including our spouses' lives and the lives of our collective five children. I soon sepa-rated from my husband, who filed for divorce. The surgeon, whom I shall call Blake, also separated from his wife. His wife moved his children to the other side of the country, and he soon followed. Before his move he broke up with me. We had many breakups. Most of them didn't last twenty-four hours before he would find me and say he didn't mean it. Over and over he would tell me he could not stay with me because of our kids, and over and over he would find me, change his mind, and I would go back to him. This was always my choice, which was one of the poorest choices in my life. I lost my power as a woman and as a human being. Blake told me, "I will love you forever. I cannot live without you. No matter what I say, no matter what I do, I will take my love for you to my grave." Dramatic, yes. This was what our relationship was all about. I can't even begin to describe how much drama there was, and I am very embarrassed by many of my actions. I was addicted to the drama and I was addicted to what I thought was love. My reality at that time was so distorted that I could no longer discern right from wrong. All I knew was that I wanted his love back at any cost. Because he left and came back so many times, I could not understand his leaving for the last time. He finally meant it. I felt as if I were going crazy.

Addictions make you do many disgraceful things. It's easy to lose your dignity and your strength. I could no longer feed my addiction, as Blake had left me. I humiliated and degraded myself trying. One evening I went to his house unannounced and he told me to go home. I felt like a lost puppy looking for love and affection. I went home, laid on the floor, and cried. I cried and cried and cried that night. I realized I had lost my dignity and my self-love. I vowed to myself that I would never try to see or contact Blake again. It was that night that I hit my lowest of lows. I remember lying on the floor in my bedroom crying and feeling as if I could not get up. I felt hopeless and so very unlovable. I laid there in my darkness for a long time wondering if I could get up and go on. I felt as if I deserved to be gang-raped in an alley. That's how bad it got and how unlovable I felt. I felt worthless. I didn't want to live anymore.

As I was lying there on the floor, something happened. A glimmer of light found its way to me. I prayed for God to help me. I knew I had two very innocent little boys, ages seven and eight, and I knew I must go on for their sake. It was my love for my boys that forced me to get up and keep going. It was at that moment my healing began. I never imagined that it was going to take twenty years, with many winding roads and many wrong turns, to finally feel whole again and find a place of peace. That peace is self-love. As I limped my way through life, I continued to grow and evolve, but very slowly.

Because of my strong addiction to what I thought was love, I continued my search to replace Blake and the family unit. I joined a dating service and dated, dated, and dated some more. One weekend I had six dates with six different men. This was not uncommon for me. I dated and discarded many men, like you would eat and toss an apple away. I felt as if I had created a giant heap of discarded men behind me. I wanted to replace what I had lost, a family unit. All of the men I dated fell short of what I thought I was looking for, so they got tossed into the heap. Some of them may have been good men, but I wasn't able to recognize this at that time, as I was looking for what I thought Blake represented to me—love and family.

During this healing time I was seeking help to repair the deep wounds of the lost love, lost family, and loss of self-love. I began my quest for help. I sought help in several ways but found that talking psychotherapy seemed to be the only thing available to me. I also looked for help from the church, but that seemed to fall short of the deeper meaning I was looking for. It was at that time that I vowed to myself, "If I get through this, I must do something to help others in similar pain. If I could just get myself out of this dark hole I feel lost in, I want to do something to give back to the many men and women in similar circumstances."

Pain is pain. It doesn't matter where it comes from. Emotional pain is a universal language. It is a feeling of hopelessness. It is like the cat trying to catch its tail. You feel as if you are going round and round, like clothes tumbling in the dryer, but you can't seem to find your way out.

My life changed again forever when my dad died of gallbladder cancer in 1992. I had just broken up with a dentist I had been dating for eighteen months and was even thinking of marrying. My dad was diagnosed with cancer in July of 1992 and died in September, only two months later. He went quickly. When the end was near, my dad had slipped into a coma. My sister Nancy and I flew from San Diego to be by my dad's side. My father lived in the San Francisco area. My sister Shirley also flew in from Australia. It was a very hard day, as my dad was breathing heavily. He was comatose, nonresponsive, and no longer eating. I sat by his side and talked to him about his favorite place on earth, a place on the coast in northern California called Sea Ranch. I led him on a guided visualization journey and talked to him about being in Sea Ranch. As I talked he seemed to get calmer, and his breathing began to slow. Being a nurse, I knew what death smelled like. I could smell this in my dad as his insides were beginning to die. My dad was a man of dignity, and my heart broke to see him in diapers and in this vulnerable state.

That evening two of my sisters went home, and my sister Shirley and I stayed by my dad's side. I feared it would be his last night. My sister and I were with my dad as he took his last breath. It came slowly. I remember his last gasp, and then it was over. I cried, held his hand, and put my head on his shoulder. His wife left the room to call hospice. I then felt a thick, loving presence enter the room. It filled the room with a cloud of love and warmth. I said to my sister, "Do you feel that?" She agreed that she did. As hospice arrived, I left the room. I remember turning back to look at my dad for the last time and I could see that he was no longer lying in his bed. It was his lifeless body lying on the bed, but my dad's spirit was gone. This was my beginning into a new understanding of body versus spirit. As time went on, I began to understand that the body is purely a home for the spirit to reside in as long as the body's cells and tissue stay alive. I will go into more detail about this later.

I slept on his couch in the living room that evening but got little sleep. My dad's spirit came to me that night. I had never experienced anything like this before. I could feel him around me and he comforted me. It was at that moment that I went from being a religious, born-again Christian, living by the rules and judgments of the church, to an awakening into "the other side" and into my spirituality. My dad came to me often after his death. It was a spiritual side of life that I never knew existed until I began to follow my dad's spirit to a very calm and beautiful place during my meditations. This is when I began to understand what a spirit was. When I went with my dad to "the other side," a place I believe spirits go after they leave their body, I always felt a presence of deep love and peace. It was like discovering a whole new existence. It was a place where beings were full of love, peace, and harmony. I experienced them as all-loving and all-giving. I realized that this was where my dad's spirit now resided. He had passed from being in his earthly body to his now eternal spirit. I believe to this day that spirits reside in this place, one that I call "the other side." They know no space and time before they choose to come into bodily form. It is also where they go when they leave their fleshly body. This is only my own personal belief and interpretation, as I have no other way to explain what I felt as I traveled there. I respect and accept each individual's theory on the matter. For me, when I visit there, I find a very beautiful and peaceful place, one unknown to the logical and scientific world.

Being a nurse and working in a scientific setting, this new experience was something that I could not logically explain. There was no concrete or scientific explanation for what I experienced as I journeyed to "the other side." I just knew it felt good and peaceful, so I went there often. It was my form of comfort. As I continued to investigate and meditate, they (my friends from the other side) started guiding me. This was the beginning of a whole new life for me, though at that time I did not understand the full extent of it. I was still healing from my broken past.

As I continued my quest into this new spiritual world, I also continued to seek love outside myself and continued my dating frenzy. In February of 1997, I met a man who I thought was the answer to my search. I will call him Eric. From the beginning Eric and I entered a whirlwind romance. It reminded me of the love I had with Blake. After two and a half months of knowing him, I asked him to move in with me. We were inseparable. I didn't acknowledge at the time that this could to be damaging to my boys. I did not put them first at this time in my life. I just wanted to create the family unit again and did this even if I had to believe in a lie and live an illusion. After all, Eric was the first man I felt really attracted to in many years. At first he seemed kind and loving, even innocent. He was an athlete and was very fit. He had competed in the Hawaiian Iron Man, and I was lured to his knowledge of fitness. That was something we strongly shared together, as I loved the gym and running. We were engaged to be married early the following year. After the engagement, things started falling apart. We had more frequent fights. He acted very erratically at times and I didn't understand it. A few months before we were to be married, the first sign of abuse emerged. We were going to a party with some of my friends. He was upset at me for something, though I never really knew why. When we arrived at my friend's house, he dropped me off and said he was going to park the car. I was walking towards the house, and I saw him drive away. I could not believe he just left me there without saying anything to me. I was so embarrassed that I didn't go into the party. Instead I walked a few miles in the rain to a gas station. This was before cell phones were popular. I called him from the 7/11 store, very upset. When he came to pick me up, I was yelling at him about leaving me. He grabbed my hair and started pushing my head into the window of the car. He was yelling irately at me, telling me I was crazy over and over again. He said I was so crazy that he didn't want to marry me. I became silent. What had just happened? Who was this man? This was not the man I was in love with and accepted into my family. For the rest of the night we didn't speak. I was frozen and scared. My illusion of my dream coming true was crashing down around me. I couldn't let my dream go. In the morning I accepted his apology, but he asked me never to speak of the incident the night before again. After that we went on as if nothing had happened, but something inside of me was unsettled. I would not allow myself to confront that unsettled feeling, though, as I knew my illusion of the happy couple and the happy family would dissolve. Remember, I was still very broken inside and had not fully healed from the hurts of my past. Eric was a Band-Aid to my past pain that I did not want to face. I did not want to lose again. I wanted to believe this was love.

As time went on, it became obvious that there were many inconsistencies in Eric's stories and in his life before he met me. He had explanations for everything, and of course I always wanted to believe him. I was too afraid not to. Through chance, I even discovered his past problems with the IRS and bankruptcy. He had many unpaid debts. Yes, I even swept this under the rug. I wanted to create my dream at any cost, even though my reality was just an illusion of what I wanted. I continued to find out many dark secrets from his past, but I was in too deep, and I was too afraid to get out.

The day before we were to be married, my mom and three sisters gathered me into a room and warned me of Eric's inconsistencies and lies. They did not trust him and felt that I was doing the wrong thing by marrying him. I continued to defend him and said, "He sometimes just gets confused about his facts." I had to continue to defend my illusions of a happily-ever-after life. My sisters said they would support me if I really loved and believed in him, but my mom maintained that she did not support the marriage.

At the rehearsal dinner, Eric did not show up. He made up a story that he got caught up with a patient. He was an ophthalmic technician. That night when he came home, he turned his back on me in bed. I remember leaving the room and getting into bed with my older sister, Shirley. She held me as I cried and told me it was all going to be all right. The next day I talked to Eric and I accepted his apology once more. I know what you are all thinking. Remember, I was still very emotionally unhealthy at this point in my life, and I was looking for something or someone else to bring me happiness, even if that someone was a lie. I was too afraid to do anything else. At that time I allowed fear to guide my life, not love.

We decided to go through with the wedding. I continued with my false belief that love would conquer all. It was on our honeymoon that the first real physical abuse came. I was trying to act sexy but he couldn't get an erection. He then slapped my face very hard and put a big laceration over my right eye, causing my head to bleed profusely. When I looked in the mirror and saw the amount of blood pouring out, all I could do was scream. I held a rag over my eye and continued to scream. The scream soon turned into a cry, which then turned into a whimper. He again told me I was crazy and he wished he had never married me as he threw his ring across the floor. I removed my ring, curled into a ball, and silently cried myself to sleep. As I awoke the next morning, I wondered, "What am I going to do now?" I had just sold my house and was waiting for my new home to finish being built. My boys were living temporarily with their dad. I knew I could not afford the new home by myself. What was I going to do? Being more scared than I had ever been in my life, I again accepted his apology and lies.

I did not go to breakfast in the main kitchen that morning. The window had been open the night before, and I was sure all of the other tenants at the bed and breakfast had heard me scream the night before. My eye was also black and blue, and I had a deep laceration over my eyebrow. I was numb. That morning we quickly got into the car and left even though we had already paid for a second night. We drove into the middle of Maine towards Moosehead Lake. Again, I was silent. It took a couple of days before I could trust Eric again, but my illusion that Eric represented all of my dreams was in the forefront of my mind and I stuffed my fear away. He said he had never hit a woman before and he vowed to never hit me again. Most of you reading this right now are saying to yourself, "Yeah, right," and you are right. I had to put my blinders on and hoped that this would never happen again.

My illusions and false beliefs could only hold up for so long, and the lies and abuse continued. That marriage lasted a year. During that year, as you can guess, there was a lot of drama and a roller-coaster ride of emotions. I was used to the ups and downs of emotions because of my time with Blake. The continuous drama seemed like a natural state to me, but there was a part of me that knew I needed and deserved better. I still didn't know how to stay grounded, though. The one thing that saved me was a little glimmer of love for myself. It started growing and I started to believe in it. I knew I couldn't let this unhealthy living situation continue, for my own sanity and for the stability of my boys. Where were my friends from "the other side"? I knew they were always with me, but it was my choice to pay attention to them or not. After a year of being married and after numerous counseling sessions, I finally gave Eric an ultimatum. I told him that if I caught him in another lie, we were through. I had to stand firm on this for myself and for my boys. When the next lie was uncovered, and you knew it would come, I asked him to move out. With much drama, he was finally gone.

After he left, I laid on my bed and started crying uncontrollably. My dream had been shattered and I found myself alone again. I felt like such a failure. I could not stop crying. I began hyperventilating. I was having a hard time breathing. I called my mom, who was staying at my sister's in San Diego. She got in the car and drove to be with me. While she was driving to my house, she had my sister Laurie, from the San Francisco area, call and stay on the phone with me until she arrived. After my mom arrived, she tried to calm me down, but the hyperventilation continued. I felt that the walls and my life were closing in around me. I finally gathered myself together and vowed, "I will never let this happen to me again."

A kind note on moms here. My mother was, and has always been there for me, even through my adult years. All of you parents out there understand this. Our kids are always our babies, even when they have kids and grandkids of their own.

After I finally gathered myself together, I went into survival mode. My family circled their wagons around me and helped me through it. Financially I was close to ruin. I was living in a home that I could not afford on one income, and Eric took me to court to try to collect spousal support. Five thousand dollars later, he was ordered to pay me a settlement of several thousand dollars, which I have not yet seen to this day. The chapter in my life with Eric had ended, and again I picked myself up, dusted myself off, and moved forward.

I went through a series of roommates to help make ends meet. I also started my journey into the athletic community. I ran many races while training for a marathon and placed in my age division in most of the races I ran. Being a strong athlete was something I could control in my life and no one could take it from me. I had complete control of how I wanted my body to perform, and it did what I told it to. All in all, I ran many 5Ks, 10Ks, many half-marathons, some triathlons, and a total of eight marathons. My goal was to run the Boston Marathon, which I accomplished in April 2004. This was my last marathon, as my body decided enough was enough. It was also at this point in my life that I understood how visualization could bring good results. I learned to focus on the end results of what I wanted. This started to work in many areas of my life, including my races. I was still growing spiritually, though, and my self-love was not fully developed. I continued to search for someone else to complete me or make me happy. You all should be saying to yourself right now, "Bad idea." Congratulations if you had those thoughts!

I met Frank on my fiftieth birthday. Our relationship started out fast and furious, and within six weeks he told me that he loved me. Frank was a kind and gentle soul and seemed to have a lot of sensitivity and love. I fell fast for him and we grew a strong bond together very quickly. Again, I did not look at the whole picture. There were many warning signs and red flags, but because of all the good qualities, I thought he was the answer to all of my prayers and that he was the man I had always dreamed of. What do you think I did with the warning signs? If you answered, "Ignored them," you are catching on.

Frank was wonderful in many ways, but as I learned with time, he had a hard time sustaining continuous love. Frank allowed fear to guide his life in many ways. He was always afraid that someone was going to take advantage of him, including me. He did not trust. He would often retreat into his cave and do or say things that made me feel unloved and unimportant. Yes, I attracted an energy that reminded me of how I felt about myself down deep—unlovable. Frank always seemed to be looking out for Frank, not Jan. I still had not taken that time to completely heal myself and find my own peace and self-love before I brought Frank into my life, so I attracted a similar energy. I was looking for love outside of myself and for a man to bring that to me. I was looking for another to make me whole. I know now, and you will learn, this never works. Frank simply reflected back to me how I truly felt about myself, not fully deserving of continuous and unconditional love. This was the reality I created.

Six months after being with Frank, the warning signs and drama began. I was on a roller-coaster ride again. I went from feeling very happy, loved, and cared for to feeling very unhappy, unloved, and unimportant. I called this "the oasis versus the desert." This was all too familiar to me. Funny that it was the exact same type of drama I had with Blake and Eric, only scaled down quite a bit. Obviously I had not learned how to stop repeating these unhealthy patterns. My lessons on how to become a whole, healthy person had not completely evolved in me yet.

This is how my life continued with Frank. After a year of dating, he moved in with me. After two more years of ups and downs, we finally married. We married even though we never really reached a healthy state of love and support for each other. When things were good, we couldn't imagine life without each other. I married him believing that if I were his wife, he would treat me better. Wrong! Three months after we were married, I told him the relationship was over and I asked him to move out.

It caused me a lot of pain to come to this decision. I loved Frank more purely than I had loved any other man. I began to get more into my spirituality and began communicating again with my friends from "the other side." I retreated back to that beautiful, peaceful place my dad took me to after his death. The gentle, accepting spirits there seemed to watch out for me and guide me. I felt as if they were telling me I needed to leave Frank and only then would I find my true happiness. I loved Frank, so by asking him to leave I stepped out in faith that what the voices were telling me was real. I was so tired of the up-and-down emotions that this relationship brought me. I needed to finally have peace. I needed to find love. I knew I deserved better, and my love for myself started growing. I could not turn back, and the support from my "spiritual helpers" gave me the strength and hope to go on. As I sought their help, I felt them around me more and more. "Seek and you shall find" seemed to bear truth at this time in my life. I continued to seek them and they continued to guide me. Some may call these helpers angels, some call them our spiritual guides but I prefer to call them my friends from the other side. As I sought to be closer to the spiritual side, the gentle spirits continued to push me forward. They felt to me like a powerful, spiritual energy that was full of love and light. I knew this spiritual energy I was feeling was part of me and part of every living thing. It was all good and all pure. It was later that I discovered this spiritual energy was within me and with me always. It is a continuous flow of love and peace. I carry this with me today.

After many tears and many attempts by Frank to contact me after our split, my heart tried to stay strong. I made it through the holidays, but in January of 2007 I was lonely again. I tried to date but could only think of Frank. I thought I missed him and never really stopped loving him. After a couple of weeks we decided to get back together. I guess I needed one last try at something I loved and believed in, and I hoped he would change. My old fears of being alone started to surface. We got back together on the condition of regularly going to continuous couple's counseling. This was to no avail. As we all know and I have proved to myself many times, "You cannot change people unless they want to change." No matter how much you love someone, it doesn't mean that it is the right and healthiest situation for you.

After five weeks of trying to salvage our relationship, situations continued to come up that gave me the same feelings of being unloved and uncared for by Frank's words or actions. What was the universe trying to tell me? It all came crashing down one day in March 2007. Frank was taking me to the airport. I was on my way to Australia to spend some time with my sister Shirley. The old saying "things happen for a reason" really held true this day. I knew my little spiritual friends had other plans for me in my life, and they worked hard to get me to hear them. On our way to the airport, Frank's words and actions again made me feel very unimportant and unloved. He complained about picking me up at the airport when I came home as it was on Easter Day at 1 p.m. and he wanted to spend that time with his family. Picking me up at 1 p.m. would interrupt his day with his family. "Why didn't you think of that when you made the reservations?" he snapped at me. I was silent, stunned, and hurt. I was still his wife. Wasn't I his family? He then dropped me off at the terminal. I got my bags out of the trunk and walked away without saying anything. I couldn't believe what had just happened, but as I know now, it was meant to be and had to be for me to be able to walk away from him for good. In my long flight to Australia, I had sixteen hours to think about it all. "I must move on" kept running through my head. It couldn't have been clearer to me. I had three weeks in Australia with my family to continue to build the clarity around what I must do. This was still very hard for me because I did feel a strong bond with Frank. This bond felt stronger than I had felt with any man before. I now know, however, that our love was not pure. It was a love of need. Because I had begun my journey of learning to love myself more, I could no longer bond with Frank's energy. This was an energy that, at times, made me feel unimportant and unlovable. I could not allow this energy around me anymore.

While in Australia, I was pondering on my final decision to leave Frank. We communicated a couple of times, but there was still that sick feeling in the pit of my stomach. My whole physical and spiritual being would not let me go back to him. At night before I went to sleep, the voices in my head wouldn't stop. I assumed they were the voices of my spiritual friends, or they could have been my own inner voice trying to guide me. The voices were relentless. They would not stop speaking to me. They spoke when I tried to sleep, when I awoke, and when I was running. Their voices would not stop, almost yelling at me to keep my attention. They were adamant at what they were telling me, and they would not let up until I finally gave in to their desires for my life. Because I could not control these voices and could not make them go away, I thought it would be a good idea to pay attention. They kept saying, "You must leave Frank. We have something so much better for you. You have a life of abundance waiting for you. You have not known this love before. It will fill you up with so much that you can't even imagine, as you have yet to feel this way. You have abundance in store for you. You must leave Frank. The world is waiting. You will step into an oasis that will take you farther than you could ever imagine. You will have a life of abundance. This we promise."

This went on for a few days until I could not ignore the voices anymore. I wrote Frank an e-mail to say my final goodbye. The next day I went for a long run around the lake. I realized my life as I knew it would again make a drastic change, as I was about to embark on a new journey. I was scared because all that I had known was about to change. It had already started. I could no longer give in to helping the wounded at the expense of myself. I knew I had to help myself get healthy and whole before I could ever truly help others find true and pure love. I knew I had to find that place of strength where I stood balanced and full of love for myself, connected to my inner spirit. I now know that it is only from that place of unlimited love that I can stand strong and no one can take it from me. That love is part of me and is always available.

On my run the day after my final goodbye e-mail to Frank, I began to cry as I was letting go. At about mile ten, I started crying so hard that I had to stop and find a place where no one could see me. I was crying uncontrollably. I had to let it all out. I had to release the past and the fear of letting go. I began to hyperventilate as I had done in the past when I had to let go of someone I thought I had loved. I had a hard time catching my breath. Somehow the panic comforted me. I knew it was a passage through an ending of one phase of my life to a new beginning. I worked through the fear, pain, and loss. As I allowed the panic to pass, I composed myself and again vowed to only go forward. I wanted to only go forward and let go of all the pain from the past. I just physically, emotionally, and spiritually could not do anything else at this point in my life but to go forward and to keep moving toward the light. There was no other choice for me. I knew I had to pick up the scared little girl inside of me and carry her to the abundance that was promised.

SPIRITUAL CONNECTION

MOVING TOWARD THE LIGHT
CONNECTING TO SPIRIT

Light is love, and love is my connection to my Inner Spirit.

When I move towards the light, I find my peace.

*When I gaze at the light, I feel a sense
of warmth and protection.*

Light is something that draws you toward it. Like a moth to a flame, light is like a magnet for those seeking a way out of darkness. Light represents all that is good, all that is pure, and all that is safe. Once you finally experience its purity, it is hard to turn away or stay away.

I'm sure all of us at some point and time in our lives have experienced a feeling of pure love or pure joy. For many it is a clean, pure feeling, and it is filled with light. On the other hand, we also seem to know what fear, anger, and darkness are. These are feelings that come from a dark and unhappy place representing fear. Fear never produces positive results other than sometimes propelling you towards something positive to move away from that which you are fearful of.

Those of you that have had a spiritual encounter understand the feeling of being in the presence of love and light. The term "God" can mean different things to many people. I use the term "God" not in the religious, church sense, but with a broader, more infinite, and all-encompassing meaning. There are many religions in this world and many ways to worship or experience God, or your inner spirit. Because this is a very sensitive topic, for the purposes of this book we shall let the meaning of God/Spirit be whatever you, the reader, understands it to be. Throughout the remainder of this book I will use the term Spirit whenever I am referring to this spiritual entity. It is always, however, an encounter with something positive. It is a feeling of love and being protected. For those of you who have tried meditation, you may understand it as even more infinite and encompassing. I respect each person's personal belief and honor your individual pursuit of what or who you perceive God/Spirit to be. Just know that when you seek the light and open to receive it, it will flow to you. The more you open to light, the more it will be available to you. When it surrounds you, there are no known human words to describe it. It is always peace. When you stand in the light, you will know you are in the presence of love and everything representative of good.

Connecting to Spirit

When I connect to my inner spirit,
I feel peace, love, and joy.

When I connect to my inner spirit, I
find balance and direction.

When I connect to my inner spirit,
I find unconditional love.

You might be wondering, "How do I move toward the Light or make a connection to Spirit?" The first step is having the desire. The second step is quieting your mind and opening your heart. I'm sure most of you have experienced tragic times in your life where you may have sought what you perceived to be Spirit or Light to find comfort and help. Spirit and Light are always available. In fact, Spirit lives within each of us, because when we came into this world, we all came from the same source of Spirit. We were connected to this source when our spirit came in as newborns. If you want to find that simple, pure peace, it is now up to you to reconnect if you feel you have drifted. I cannot overstress to you how beautiful that reconnection can be. I cannot think of human words or terms to describe the feeling of being in the presence of this light other than the old cliché terms such as "love," "peace," and "harmony." When I connect to this light, it feels as if I am being cleansed in a state of euphoria. It is always there, and once accessed, it becomes familiar and easier to make a part of your daily existence.

As you may recall, when my father died I felt his spirit requesting me to join him. Because I missed him, I followed him in my mind to where he now resides, on "the other side." Many may think of "the other side" as a representation of what they perceive heaven to be. For me, I learned there are no rules, no judgments, and no such thing as what the church defines as sin or hell. From visiting the other side and learning from my spiritual friends, I became aware that we are all spirits, or energy, derived from the same source. We come into this world to find our way. We come to learn, grow, and evolve. When I visit the other side, I know that it is a place I can also call home. I hope this does not sound too overbearing but I am speaking from my heart and only from my own personal experience. By turning towards the light, you too can find your way home. It will help you to remember who you really are, and eventually the everyday cares of this world may seem small. You will be able to see a bigger picture and become part of this bigger picture as you allow your inner voice, which is connected to your infinite spirit, to guide you.

It is now my desire to share with you a pathway guiding you towards your connection to your infinite being. The tools needed to fulfill this are simple. All you need to get started is a desire and the willingness to quiet your mind and open your heart. When I say "quiet your mind and open your heart," you may wonder how to do this. If you are not in the practice of doing this, when you first try it your mind may be full of thoughts and chatter. Simply get yourself in a relaxed position. You may put on some relaxing music. If you find yourself struggling to relax, it may help to take some deep breaths and see yourself releasing the chatter in your mind as you exhale. If the chatter in your head continues, just move it to the side of your mind and continue to focus on your breathing. Imagine that with each breath you take, you become more and more relaxed. As you become more and more relaxed, imagine yourself moving into a very calming light. Ask for it to come to you. As you move toward it you should feel a sense of lightness, beauty, and calmness. It can become all-encompassing. Continue to breath and allow yourself to bathe in the light. Move away from your thoughts. The light will become love and you will feel oneness with it. Allow it to be in you. It will be a place you will not want to leave and a place you will want to visit often. It is your source of universal love and self-love. It is your source of guidance. It is all-fulfilling. You can tap into it at anytime and anywhere. It is within all of us. We were all born as part of this light. It will comfort you. It will teach you the meaning of true, pure love without expectations or judgments. It will help to bring clarity in your life. Once you have tapped into your inner spirit and light, it will continue to be your source of power and enable you to create a life of abundance that you have always dreamed of. You can now gain control and be the director in every aspect of your life. You are the director, and the world is your screenplay. This point of connecting to your inner peace or inner spirit is important as it will set you up with a foundation that guides you and helps you find your way to happiness. This foundation will also help you to navigate through the pages that follow.

MAKING CHOICES—
CREATING YOUR LIFE

*I now make choices that are in perfect alignment
with my soul desire and purpose, bringing more
peace and harmony into my life.*

There may be times in your life that you are conflicted about
a choice you are about to make. Which way should you

go, to the right or to the left? Through quieting your mind or using the tools of meditation, you have now learned how to connect to your source, your inner light, which loves and guides you. You can now have better clarity when you ask the questions "Which way should I go?" or "Which choice should I make?" The key now is to relax, listen, and allow the answer to show itself to you. This requires you to pay attention to your surroundings and what is presented in front of you each day.

A good way to gauge whether you want to choose choice A or choice B is to listen to what your inner emotions are telling you. This is often referred to as listening to your intuition, your inner voice, or, for men, listening to your gut feelings. If you choose this way to look for answers, it helps to go to the place of peace and quiet in your mind as I have described in the previous chapter. First, get comfortable and quiet your mind. Ask the chatter in your head, if there is any, to move aside, and then enter a place in your mind that brings you calmness. You can do this anywhere and in any place. The more you do this, the easier it is to access. Just take a small time-out to review the questions and choices that are before you. After you have become relaxed and your mind quieted, bring the choices you have questions about to stand before you in your mind. Imagine yourself following one of these choices. Allow yourself time to be with this choice. Observe how it makes you feel. Does it make you feel happy and joyful, or does it make you tense and upset? Now, do the same for the other choice or choices. Spend time with each one. Play out in your mind what it would look like or feel like if you moved in either direction. If you pay attention to your emotions and how you are feeling with each particular choice, you will have your answer. Always move toward the direction that makes you feel happy and light and you will be on your right path.

As you learn to connect with Spirit and your Light, you will find more peace in your life. If you ask for guidance, it will always come. It may not come in the form you think it should, but pay attention and "follow the bread crumbs" as they arrive in your life. This term "follow the bread crumbs" is simply a fun way to acknowledge divine guidance when it shows up for you. Bread crumbs could come in many forms, such as people, places, or things all coming together to create magic. If you pay attention and look beyond the surface of the little things in your life, you will see your path and you will see your bread crumbs guiding you forward. When I see or acknowledge the sign of bread crumbs laying out a path before me, I always get excited because I know it is a sign that I am being guided by my spiritual friends. It is also a sign that I am creating my life just the way I want it. The bread crumbs represent to me that my purpose in life is unfolding. It is a representation of my faith, my hopes, and my dreams becoming my reality.

THE POWER OF THOUGHTS

My thoughts are always positive, bringing more peace, harmony, and abundance into my life.

I focus my thoughts on appreciation and my life's desires.

I understand that my thoughts create my future, so I only focus on what I want my life to look like. I am thankful for all that I have.

I am the creator of my reality through my thoughts.

As I have discussed earlier, you can create any outcome you desire through your thoughts and life choices. As we think thoughts and attach a strong emotion to them, it will bring that situation much faster to us. Can you think of a time when this may have happened to you? Think of a time when you attached a lot of emotion to a thought. How long did it take before that thought showed up as reality in your life? What you think about, speak about, and see in your mind is creating your future. It then becomes your choice to create exactly what you want with your mind. Positive thoughts will lead to a positive experience in your future. Negative thoughts will bring just that, more negative experiences. Take a second now and think about what your thoughts have been over the past month, weeks, or days. Now think about how you currently feel or what you currently see in your life. Does it match what you have been thinking about?

A powerful time when our thoughts can penetrate and assist in creating our reality is the time just before we go to sleep and the time just as we awake. What you think about before you go to sleep is usually what's on your mind when you wake up. You have allowed those thoughts, good or bad, to soak into your subconscious throughout your relaxed sleep time. How do you think these thoughts will set up the next day when you awake? When I go to sleep at night, isn't it funny that I awake continuing the same discussion that I had with myself the night before? Sometimes I go to sleep with a melody or song in my head, only to awake continuing to sing the same song. So, as you can see, our thoughts before we sleep become very powerful. They stay with us for a number of hours and for many of us can set the stage for all that we draw to us in the days to come.

Your thoughts in the morning are equally as powerful. These morning thoughts again can set the tone for what your day will look like. Knowing this gives you the power to control it. Be aware of what you think about when you go to sleep and when you awake. It is always good to start and end each day with thanks and appreciation. As I will repeat many times, the more we appreciate, the more we will have to appreciate in our lives. Do you think you would have a different outcome during the day if you started with thoughts of anger, resentment, and judgment? Try awaking with positive thoughts and continue feeling positive and thankful throughout the day. Then see how you feel as you sleep that evening. It should be more restful. Your next day will also attract to you more to be thankful for. Just try this for a day, a week, and maybe a month. Once you get into the habit of being positive, you will see a change in your life and your health. You will not want to go back to giving energy to scarcity or negativity. This is your life and your choice.

As you create this new, positive life for yourself by simply changing your thought process, you will see a change towards a happier, more fulfilled life. Once you have mastered this, just relax and allow fun things to show up on their own terms. You no longer need to force things or events into being. You can now trust. When you stop trying to control everything in your life and learn to relax, allow, trust, and go with the flow, you will see your desires come to you in their own perfect timing. I will discuss this further in the "Trust" chapter.

You may now be saying to yourself, "How can I change and create my life just through my thoughts"? It may sound strange at first, but when you start moving toward more positive thoughts, it is amazing how you feel and what shows up in your life during the next few days, months, or years.

We all have certain statements or phrases that we think about or say frequently. It is interesting when the reality of our lives matches the phrases we say. Below are some random examples of negative phrases. See if any of them sound familiar to you. You can even insert your own phrases if you can identify some that you often think of or worry about.

- I can never find a parking spot.
- I can never find a good seat in the movie theatre, or someone always kicks my seat from behind.
- My left knee and back hurt every morning.
- I always attract unavailable partners.
- I am fat.
- I never have enough money.
- I get sick easily.
- I always attract crazy or controlling partners.
- I feel lonely.
- My partner is unappreciative of me.
- My kids always talk back to me and are out of control.
- I am not attractive.
- My car always breaks down.
- My life is boring.

This list can go on and on, but I think you are getting the picture here. It was actually very hard for me to write the above statements, because I have created a habit of only thinking positive and uplifting thoughts. It is now very uncomfortable for me to have negative thoughts. You may see yourself in some of the above statements. Can you see that by continually saying and believing each statement, it starts to create the day-to-day story of your life?

Now comes the fun part. I will change each statement into a positive one.

- I always find the perfect parking spot.
- When I go to the movies or theatre, I always have a great and comfortable seat.
- Every morning when I arise, I feel healthy and energized. My body is strong and ready for a wonderful day.

- I have a man/woman in my life that is physically, emotionally, and spiritually available. He/she loves and cares for me every day, and we have a balanced circle of giving and receiving.
- I have a beautiful and fit body that I am very proud of.
- I always have more money than I need to have everything I want. I live a life of abundance.
- My body is healthy in mind, body, and spirit.
- I have a beautiful and loving man/woman in my life, and we respect and appreciate each other.
- I freely give and receive love. I feel loved and I am lovable.
- My partner accepts, loves, and appreciates me, and I easily give back in return. We have a harmonious and balanced relationship.
- My children are healthy and respectful to those around them and are full of integrity. I have a healthy, loving, and respectful relationship with my children. My children are healthy, happy, and successful. They treat others with respect and dignity.
- I am beautiful/handsome and love the way I look. I have beautiful, healthy skin and a beautiful body.
- My car runs forever and always takes me safely from one destination to another.
- I have an exciting, fun, and adventurous life.

Did you notice a difference in how you felt when you read these positive statements? Can you imagine how you would feel if you said positive affirmations to yourself daily?

Try reading the negative statements again, and notice how they make you feel. Now read the positive ones again. Change your own personal thoughts or phrases you identified to positive ones. Don't you feel a sense of relief when you turn your thoughts to a more positive form? You can do this in all areas of your life. Pay attention to your thoughts. When they come out negative, quickly change them to positive ones like I have shown you. You will be amazed how much better you will feel and how simple thoughts can change the story of your life. This is self-empowerment and an example of you taking control of your life. It is your life and your choice. There is no need to be unhappy or unhealthy anymore. Change your thoughts and change the circumstances in your life.

TAKING RESPONSIBILITY

**I take full responsibility for my life and
how I have created it.**

I forgive myself and others from my past.

I have the power to create my life just the way I want it.

It is important that we take responsibility for our own out-comes in our lives. When you take a personal inventory of who you are and what you have in your life today, you can now say, "I have created it all." When you move into adult-hood, it is time to stop blaming others for what you have created. It is now time to take responsibility for it all. If you think someone has done something to you that made you sad or angry, think again. Who actually has the power to feel these emotions? No one other than you has the power to feel an emotion. Sure, someone may do something that evokes an emotion, but it is always our own choice as to how we act or react to any situation. I could look back on my life and say, "Blake did this or that to me. He promised me he would love me forever and then he left. Because he left me, I felt empty and very sad." Actually, it was my choice to continue to go back to Blake even though I knew it would only cause me sorrow. It was my choice to feel empty and sad. It was also my choice to get out of those negative feelings and instead create something positive in my life.

We each have the power to create our own personal inner peace. There is no reason to stay stuck or feel trapped in any situation anymore in your life. You need to understand that if you stay, it is your choice; if you leave, it is your choice; if you feel empty or sad, it is your choice; and if you change your circumstances and thoughts to be more positive, it is also your choice. Congratulations if you choose self-empowerment, freedom, and happiness.

✓ Note to reader: There are many more topics related to self-empowerment to come. As you read further, you will notice that I get less airy-fairy and more in your face. This is only to push you further as I take you deeper into your own self-discovery. Hang on; you can get through this. I believe in you, so now it is time for you to be completely honest with yourself, believe in yourself, and trust.

STANDING AT THE CROSSROADS

*I have positive thoughts when I go to
sleep and when I awake.*

*Positive thoughts today bring about a
more positive tomorrow.*

I live a life full of balance, peace, and harmony.

By now, many of you reading this may have spent some
time reviewing your life. Some may have identified with situations from my story or may have your own story of "out of

darkness into light." Others may have been on a journey of self-growth and self-discovery for some time. As you have been reexamining your life, there may be some questions still worth paying attention to. Are you happy with what you have taken notice of thus far? Do you feel appreciation each night before sleep and in the morning when you awake? What do you find yourself thinking about most of the time? Are they positive thoughts and beliefs? If this doesn't describe you, then you may want to change some circumstances in your life or change the way you think about them.

We all know people who are always negative. They are difficult to be around, as they are always complaining about one thing or another. Have you ever noticed that they are never happy? How do you think their thoughts have created their reality? We also have known people who seem to have a lot of chaos around them, or continuous drama. That chaotic energy continues to attract more chaos and more drama. Chaos and drama seem to magnetize themselves easily to those that continue to give them energy. Let's personalize this now. For those who have identified with continuous drama, how do you get out of this? First you have to want to end the drama. Once you have taken the first step of realizing your life is spinning out of control and you have a desire for it to stop, you have taken your first baby step toward a more peaceful life. The more you seek peace, the more peace will find you. The "drama people" (we have now impersonalized it) need to stop spinning in that energy, as this just reinforces the chaos and it soon becomes a way of life for them. They feel comfortable in it because it has become habitual and familiar. I understand this, as I lived it for many years with a life of ups and downs. My roller-coaster ride of emotions felt normal for so many years because it became a habit of my day-to-day existence. I didn't know how to get out of it, but I knew it was uncomfortable. I knew down deep that there must have been a better, more peaceful way to live. It was not until I said, "Wait, I want to get off," that the ride started to slow down. I had to change my thoughts, choices, and actions in order for the drama and chaos to slowly go away. Yes, as you read in my story, it was a slow but steady course. I sought peace, and the peace that was always within surfaced.

The question arises now, how do you change this, and how do you remove drama and chaos from your life once you have acknowledged its existence? It takes time to change habits. I had to change familiar, long-term habits in my life. I began by changing my thought process from negative to continuously positive. I also had to learn to love myself. This was difficult at first, but when I sought my inner peace, I found my inner love. Changing my thoughts to more positive and uplifting ones took effort at first, but as time went on it started to become a more natural way of thinking and being. The first three months, being aware of my thoughts seemed to be constant work. As the months went by, it started to become easier. It actually then became hard to be in a negative space. Negativity was not aligned with my new self. It also became harder to be around negative or emotionally unhealthy people. This was new for me, because in my previous existence I was emotionally unhealthy. It was no surprise, then, that the people I drew in and around me were also emotionally unhealthy. I became a new, healthy being that understood I was lovable and deserved to be loved. Circumstances or people in my life that reflected otherwise were no longer attractive to me. Because of the new self I was creating, I now seemed to repel drama and chaos as it came near me. I wasn't attracting it to me as I had in the past. When unhealthy energy came around me, it felt uncomfortable. Before I made the conscious decision that I wanted change, drama and chaos found its way to me, and it felt common and familiar. As my life became more stable and my desire for self-love and inner peace matched my core existence more, I then began to recognize my drama before it started spinning out of control.

If you, like me, have led a life with a lot of past drama, just know that you will be tested as you wean yourself away from these patterns. When I started to connect to a drama event, or a drama individual, I could feel it was wrong for my life through the inner turmoil I was feeling inside. Something just didn't feel right. Something inside of me said, "When I engage with this situation or person, it does not make me feel happy or peaceful." Once recognized, I knew to remove myself from the person or situation that was causing my inner conflict. To put it boldly, and you have to be strong, I terminated them. This can be challenging, but pay attention to how you are feeling. When you move away from a person or situation that is causing you to have uncomfortable feelings, you may then notice how happy and light you feel.

Following your feelings is all part of following your "bread crumbs." As discussed previously, your inner feelings will let you know if you are on the right path. When you are searching for self-love, inner peace, and true harmony in your life, your inner being and outer body will let you know when you have made the right choices by your emotions or physical manifestations. Insomnia, anxiety, fearfulness, and self-doubt are all manifestations of a wrong choice or wrong situation you have put yourself in. Choose a different direction and you will notice a difference in how you are feeling. If you are now sleeping better, feel happy and light during the day, and have an inner glow within you, then you know you have made a good choice. You will feel in alignment with the new you and the new life you have now chosen to create.

There may be situations you have in your life that you are unable to remove yourself from because of responsibilities and family ties. These may include life situations such as work, school, or family responsibilities. When you are unable to move away from a person or situation because he, she, or it is permanently in your life, it helps to then change the way you see or think about the person or situation. If you are in a relationship with someone and you feel unhappy, it might help to change the way you think about this person. You can begin by thinking of all the ways you appreciate him or her. Everyone has something that is positive to acknowledge. Start seeing and thinking about all of the things you appreciate and love about the person. It is amazing how quickly this can change the tone of the relationship. It can change the person's actions towards you as well. Love does move mountains. When you give love out, it finds its way back to you. The same holds true of anger and offensive behavior. Anger never has a good outcome and only promotes defensiveness and more of what you are unhappy about. Try giving love, acceptance, and appreciation, and you will be amazed how it can diffuse an unhappy situation to renew the love and respect that was there from the beginning.

This change in the way you think also helps when you find yourself in a situation you must stay in due to responsibilities. This could be in the form of a job, school, or a responsibility that seems difficult to continue. When you change your thoughts about the situation and begin to focus on the outcome of why you are maintaining that responsibility, you begin to focus on the positive, and suddenly the unhappy situation isn't so bad. New and wonderful things could start to emerge just because you changed the way you thought about the situation. The responsibility then becomes a means to an end, and the end result is what you have chosen to have in your life. If this is not the end result you really want in your life, then change your story. Only focus on what you want instead of what you have or do not have that makes you unhappy. Stay in a positive frame of mind and keep your eye on the prize. The prize is your dream life, which represents your goals and desires for your life. As you stay focused on your end result, you will attract it to you. Stay focused, stay positive, and stay the course. Your life will start changing as you allow it to come to you. Soon you will find your reality looking exactly like what you have been dreaming of and envisioning.

When you see this shift and notice yourself feeling happier, you know you are moving in the right direction. What is the "right" direction? I believe this is your path to enlightenment and your own personal journey towards abundance, freedom, and happiness. It may also be the path towards your life's destiny.

Your heart and emotions will always let you know whether you have made the right choice or not. We all have the answers within us. Pay attention to the way you are feeling with each choice, situation, or person you let into your life. You know that if you feel happy and joyful, then you have made the right decision.

The old saying "go with the flow" is a common one and does ring true. When you are going with the flow of life, you are moving forward with the guidance of a comfortable energy force. There may even be "bread crumbs" involved. Have you ever tried to fight the flow and force yourself against it? How did it turn out? I suspect not in your best interest. I always like to use the open door/closed door theory. When a door is closed, it is for a reason. It is a red light telling you "do not enter." It is best to always choose the open path, the one of least resistance, the one with the green light. There will be your flow. Allow that to guide you through. The minute you meet resistance, you know you have made a wrong turn somewhere and you will need to readjust your course. You will know when you get back into the flow again. You will feel a calmness and peace around you. You will feel happy.

The exception to this is when depressed individuals stay frozen and have no desire to move past the resistance of getting better. These people have allowed themselves to stay in the flow that has created their own downward spiral. Many stay stuck due to their fears. They have created their own closed and locked doors and feel safe hiding behind them. They may need encouragement and guidance from emotionally healthier individuals to move past their fears and through their resistant flow that they have created. Once they are able to move out of their dark space and find some gleam of hope and light they may then find themselves back in a positive flow propelling them forward. Again, all it takes is their desire and intent to get better. Each step gets easier as they move past their own negative flow into that which is more positive. They too can then begin creating their own form of abundance for their life as they identify their goals and desires.

Remember, you don't have to have a fancy home, fancy car, and a lot of money to have abundance. Abundance could simply mean peace and happiness in your life. It is a warm and safe feeling in your heart. It is a feeling of contentment and being thankful for all that you have that can take you to a state of living in abundance. You will feel full. If you feel pure love for yourself, then you live in abundance. If you connect to this love and light, you will always have a feeling of self-love and fulfillment.

In contrast, it is good to acknowledge those around you who have less. They are fighting just for survival. There are many in this world fighting to just stay alive, struggling for food, clean water, and shelter. They are also fighting diseases that could be preventable if they had the proper health care. Many here in America and in other industrial countries have material abundance. Just look around you. Be thankful for all that you have, and you will in turn have more to be thankful for. The more you give out to those less fortunate and in need, the more abundance will return to you. Pay attention and follow your bread crumbs to the life you have always dreamed of, leading you towards emotional abundance filled with personal contentment. This is truly the foundation of pure happiness that material abundance cannot sustain.

LETTING GO

*I have let go of the past and allow all that
is good to come to me now.*

*I trust that all that comes to me is for my best interest when
I visualize my desires and let go of attachments.*

As you have read in my story, I have had to do a lot of letting go in my past. Most of my letting go was in the form of

letting go of a relationship. Many of us have experienced having to let go of something or someone we love. It is quite painful, because most of the time we are attached to the person or thing we have had to let go of. We become use to having them or it in our lives. It is never easy. A slow, steady, progressive process of letting go, allowing yourself time to heal, usually turns out for the better. There is always a transition period of adjusting to life without this person or thing. When you love or are attached to someone or something in your life, it doesn't matter whether this was healthy for you or not, it is still something that felt familiar and comfortable being in your life. If one day you wake up to find it gone, there is always a process of grieving and letting go. If you skip this process and quickly attach to someone or something else, you have stuffed away your grief and sorrow, and it will surely come out again in other forms. I do believe your pain and sorrow will not leave you unless you allow yourself time to go through the grieving process. A lot of people want to run from this pain. They look for someone or something else to fill them up with happiness to avoid the pain of grieving. I did this for years when I ended my first marriage. This rarely turns out well. We need to make our own selves whole and not expect another to fill us up or make us happy. If you don't have that fulfillment and happiness within yourself, no person or thing can replace that for you. If you are looking for someone or something outside of yourself to make you happy, you have just set yourself up for disappointment, because that happiness is usually not sustained over time.

There are many examples of this. One very obvious one is what many people do at the end of a relationship. They became attached to a person they now have to let go of and live without in their lives. I have learned through experience that trying to replace this person too quickly rarely ends well. When you do this, you are just looking for someone else to comfort you and fill you up rather than looking inside and finding your own self-love and self-worth. Someone else can never do this for us. Eventually that person will fail. We can easily blame others and make excuses in our mind that they just weren't what we needed. It becomes "their fault" that we are unhappy and that they failed us. What do you really think happened here? If you took time away from a relationship to grieve and find your own inner peace, you would still be standing firm when another did not meet your expectations. When you stand firm in yourself, no one can ever cause you pain. You have the power to continue to stand strong by yourself.

We all have control over how we react to a situation. No one else makes us feel pain. It is within our own self that we create this emotion, and it is within our power to comfort ourselves and release this pain. There is never a need to be lonely or feel alone. You can be your own best friend, as you are with yourself wherever you go. Only you know how to treat yourself well, so ask yourself, "Are you caring for you?" If the answer is no or maybe, then take some time and think of things you could do for yourself to find comfort and to make yourself happy. You have this power. Who else knows you better? When you expect someone else to make you happy, he/she will fail every time, because someone else can never know exactly what you want at every minute. Others are living their lives through their own stories and creating their own happiness or unhappiness. If you let them become your strength, when they tumble, you will tumble with them.

ATTACHMENTS

I think it is important to speak about attachments at this point. What is an attachment? Attachment is holding on to something or someone very tight and not wanting to let go. You may become fearful that if you let go you could lose your balance. You may also feel that this something or someone is the only key to your happiness. Feeling this way leads to an unhealthy attachment. This could also come in the form of an attachment to a certain outcome of a situation. You may believe that if a specific outcome doesn't go the way you are expecting, your life as you know it, or hope it to be, will not be good. This is only setting yourself up to fail. When you become too attached, you give away your freedom.

The opposite of attachment is trust. When you are living in perfect harmony with your inner self, you trust that all that comes to you is for your better good. You do have control of this, though, as you dream and imagine what you want. Through your thoughts, you are creating what you want for your life. As you let go of all that you are attached to and keep your vision of what you want, you then will create a vacuum for all that you desire to flow to you in a form that is in the best interest of your soul purpose. Remember, you can envision an elephant coming your way, and before you know it you will come face to face with an elephant of some form. What you think about shows up in your reality. When you let go of attachments but keep open to your dreams, you must then trust that all that comes your way is for your better good. Accept and appreciate what comes, but stay open and unattached to outcomes. There will lay your freedom.

STAGES OF GRIEF

I have allowed myself to go through the stages of grief in a healthy manner, and I am now free to experience my new and exciting life as a whole and healthy being.

There are many theories that describe the stages of grief. My favorite is the grieving stages described by Elisabeth Kubler-Ross many years ago. She explained that when you are first confronted with the reality that you have lost someone or something you loved or felt attached to, your initial reaction is usually one of shock and disbelief. If this loss is sudden, the feeling of initial shock is even more prominent.

At first you can't imagine that this loss actually happened. You are waiting for someone to tell you it was all a mistake. You sink into denial. You simply don't want to believe it. The thought of losing that special someone or something may feel unbearable. Your initial denial can keep you feeling numb for a time, but eventually you will need to move into the next stage, which is acknowledgment that this loss has actually occurred. This may cause you to initially withdraw from your usual daily activities. This first stage of grief could last just a few moments, or may last longer.

The next stage of grieving comes in the form of anger, suffering, and depression. After you have accepted that this loss actually did take place, you may feel angry and want to blame someone. "Why did this happen to my loved one?" "Why did my loved one leave me?" "Why did I lose my job?" "Could this have been preventable?" At this point you may feel helpless because you are unable to undo this tragic outcome. You may slip into a depression, which could manifest itself in emotional as well as physical forms. During this time you may withdraw from life's responsibilities all together. This becomes a time to feel deep levels of sadness. As the pain sets in, weakness, crying, and aimlessness may occur, together with a loss of appetite, fatigue, and insomnia. This stage of grieving will hopefully only last for a short time so that you can move into the next stage, which is acceptance.

When the anger, sadness, and mourning begin to disappear, you begin to accept the reality of the loss. You are slowly able to move on with your life and become engaged with other people and activities again. At this stage, the pain may not be completely gone, but you may at least be able to function and reconnect to the healthy and happy parts of your life. You begin to live again and new beginnings start forming.

People experience these stages of grief in their own individual ways. They can also get stuck in a stage such as depression and not move on. Often people don't want to feel the pain of loss, so they suppress this emotion and try relentlessly to find something or someone to replace their loss. I did this for years until I finally came to a place where I could no longer run from my feelings of loss of self. Instead of experiencing a healthy grieving process, people may stay in denial and look for fulfillment or happiness from external sources. I know you know the correct answer to this by now. Self-love as well as treating yourself with kindness and dignity is the path to true healing.

Take time out to find your way through the pain. Treat yourself well and nurture yourself. Eat well, exercise, and be around people that love and support you. If you don't take the time to heal and come out the other side a whole being, you will continue to set yourself up for failure and disappointments as you look for someone or something else to make you happy. Remember, when the sun sets you can always count on a new day to bring you new opportunities for living a fulfilled life. Each ending brings a new beginning for you to embrace and create your life just the way you want it.

SINGLE AND DATING

*I am a whole and healthy being, and therefore
attract only whole and healthy beings into my life.*

I only allow loving and caring beings into my inner circle.

*I have attracted the perfect partner and now have
a loving, harmonious relationship full
of understanding and balance.*

I was only thirty-five when my fourteen-year marriage to the
father of my boys ended. Since then, I have dated a multi-
tude of men and attempted several short-term relationships,

more actually than I would like to admit. Yes, I was searching, and yes, I made many wrong choices along the way. I would like to call that era of my life my "past life" in this lifetime, as I now have evolved into allowing light, faith, hope, and my inner intuition to guide me. I too used to be ruled by a fear of being alone or of being unlovable. I dated many men looking for someone to help me feel whole. I am now living in a world I have created, ruled by love, hope, and trust.

It is because of this that I would love the opportunity to share with you, through my trials and errors, what I have learned about being single and dating. Get comfortable, because this is going to be a fun adventure, one which I believe many of you who are or have spent time being single can relate to. The platform from which I speak comes from my voice as a heterosexual woman. I may use the terms "men" and "women," but I do understand there are variations to this theme in loving partnerships. It is not my intention to offend anyone, as there may be many differences in our beliefs and desires for relationships. Please insert your life situation to that which best suits you, as I accept and support all that is love.

If you are currently single and are dating, then we can assume you are searching for love and/or companionship. You may be searching for that ever-elusive but attainable soul mate and may be looking for that someone to "complete you." This is a famous line that came out of the Tom Cruise movie *Jerry Maguire*. It happened when the leading man finally came back to the leading woman and said, "You complete me." Many women loved this line, because it seemed to fulfill their dreams that a man on a shining white horse was going to come in, scoop them up, and save and protect them through life. It exaggerated the notion that if you met this special person, you would finally be complete and you would live happily ever after.

Well, let's think about this for a moment. Who completes who? Yes, you are right if you arrived at the answer "I complete myself." I don't think it's all about self, but I do believe you must be a whole, healthy individual with self-love in order to be a healthy partner in a relationship. If you are looking for someone else to complete you, you will find yourself disappointed every time. How can another person complete you? Other people are on their own journeys with their own desires, goals, and individual personality characteristics. They must find their own self-love and completion. To put it simply, if you are looking for your own completion by another, what happens if that other leaves you or is not around? Do you topple over? Is this healthy? Wouldn't you rather stand firm on your own, regardless of who comes and goes in your life? Depending on another to make us happy could be very disappointing because someone else can never know exactly what we want and be there to give it to us at every moment. Our own true happiness comes from our own self-love, which I will get into in more depth later. Creating your own true peace and happiness is the best way to be a healthy, giving individual in a relationship that has a harmonious flow of giving and receiving. When you stand firm and strong on your own, with an abundance of your own self-love, you can't help but make healthy choices as to what or whom you bring into your life.

Now let's talk about dating some more. I first must speak to the females out there. Ladies, please!!!!! Let me put it to you very simply. If he's not calling and not pursuing you, then he's just not interested. It's as simple as that. This makes it very easy for you, because you can then move on and allow yourself to meet the "right" partner who is interested in you and will create a more fulfilling relationship with you. Why do you want something that is not available? This will only set you up for rejection and can only cause hurt. You are worth more than this. You are a beautiful being who deserves to love and be loved. Remember this. If a man is not available, he's not available. Don't beat down a door that is closed. This will only lead to disappointments, and you don't need that. Move through the open doors and the green lights. It makes life so much easier and happier. It creates a life of trust and harmony.

Another thing, ladies: this is only from my own personal perspective, but don't give away your most personal, private parts so easily. They should be sacred to you and only shared with the man who is deserving and who shows love and appreciation for you. You all know what I mean. If he thinks you're worth it, and you are, and if he is in it for the long haul, he will wait. Let him wait, and let it be beautiful when you finally share this sacred bond of sexual intimacy together. You should never wonder if he's going to call you the next day. If you have any doubt about this, then wait for the man who gives you his trust. Once you finally reach that trusting, emotional bond together, as you become one through intimacy, your souls will unite. Intimacy becomes a beautiful act when done out of love, trust, and unity.

There is an age-old saying that "men like the chase." This may sound old-fashioned, but ladies, this is a male instinct that seems to have been around since the caveman days. It even exists in the animal kingdom, where many of the male species are brightly colored or have more distinct physical characteristics to attract a mate. These males may also do specific attention-getting behavior to swoon a desired female into submission. The males may strut their stuff, sometimes with strength and force, to attain the chosen female they want to mate with. Women can learn from these mating rituals seen in animals by understanding the innate desire a male has to be with a female. It has happened throughout the beginning of time with all the male species. Why disrupt this balance? Most men have this drive. It is their natural instinct, driven by their desire to mate. Don't take this from them by being the aggressor. It will turn them off and turn them away almost every time. Allow the man to come to you. If he is interested, he will come. Ladies, trust me, they can't help but come. A man will do whatever it takes to win you over if this is his desire. If it is not his desire, you will know this by his actions. Relax and wait. Allow what is meant to be, to be. Trust me, I've tried it the hard way. It doesn't bring good results. Seeing in your mind what you want, trusting it will come, and allowing yourself to be open to it when it arrives gives you all the power to have whatever it is you desire. This power should give you peace. Never accept less than what you think you deserve.

Men, it is now your turn. If she is not answering you back or responding to your attempts to be with her, she is also just not interested. This should then give you the freedom to move on to a more suitable partner. You also deserve to be loved and respected by a woman. Don't allow yourself anything less than to be with a woman who loves and accepts you for who you are right now. Love is an equal partnership, and someone trying to control or change another has no place in a loving, harmonious relationship.

To both men and women; if you meet someone and think he/she would be just perfect if they would only change something about themselves, think again. They may change for a time, but usually this is in the initial honeymoon stage of a relationship. If the change is really not who the person is, he/she will only revert back to their original self, the person they were before they met you. Love him/her for who they are now, and ask yourself, "Can I live with this person without ever expecting him/her to change?"

Men seek respect and acceptance from their partners. Women seek to be cared for and cherished by their partners. When these patterns exist in a relationship, they are the foundation of a healthy, lasting partnership. If there is trouble or unhealthy disagreements in a relationship during the dating phase, this is usually a warning sign that something is not right. When issues come up, you both should be able to resolve them in a healthy, respectful, and timely fashion. If this is not happening and there is continuous fighting, this should be a warning sign to you that you may not be compatible. It may also mean that one or both of you have not learned how to have that healthy relationship with yourself yet. If one person is not whole or is unbalanced, it usually spills over into the partnership. Couple's counseling may be helpful, but I raise a big red flag here. If the problems are so insurmountable during the dating phase that you have to go to couple's counseling, just know that things can only get worse during a marriage. I have learned this firsthand through my last two short marriages. We had many problems and went to extensive couple's counseling while still dating. Obviously it didn't help, as all of the problems came back even stronger once we were married. If you are in couple's counseling and still dating, I would suggest you continue to date for a while to make sure the problems have been ironed out before getting married.

Men and women, when you are seeking a partner' you may have a list of all the qualities you are looking for in your mind or on paper. I ask you to review your "want list." Do you possess the qualities you are asking for in a mate? Just know you will attract to yourself that which you are. If you desire certain qualities or characteristics in your partner, it is important that you have many of those qualities yourself. If you have an emotional hurt from your past and are looking for a whole, healthy individual to take away that hurt, just know you will only attract another hurting individual looking for the same. This relationship can never stand firm, because neither party is standing strong on his/her own from the beginning. At times, this relationship may work as each partner gains his/her own self-worth, but many times the relationship could turn toxic, and more hurt will come your way.

I urge you to become what you are looking for. Find yourself through love and become strong and healthy on your own before you try to bring in that life partner. If your desire is for a life partner, once you have mastered this love for yourself, stay steadfast on your dreams and desires. See yourself with that special someone. See the two of you doing the things you love to do. Feel your love for each other as you think about yourselves together. Believe that you are lovable and love will find you. Never give up. Continue to see your dreams. Believe them, feel them, and allow your dream life to flow to you.

A WORD ON
RELATIONSHIPS—THE CIRCLE

*I have a wonderful, stable, harmonious
relationship full of love, caring, giving, and understanding.*

My partner and I are each other's best friends and lovers.

*I have an equal balance of giving and receiving in my
partnership, and we are very happy together.*

In my relationship there is trust, respect, stability, and harmony.

My partner and I appreciate each other daily.

If you have found that special someone to share your life with and have the kind of relationship in which you support each other and have harmony together, you have been blessed, and it is important to appreciate each other every day. I really believe the key word in making relationships work and become long lasting is appreciation, appreciation, appreciation. We all know of, or may have been in, a relationship where we felt unappreciated. It can become a vicious cycle and a very unhappy place to be. When you stop feeling appreciated, you may feel unloved and uncared for. Does that make you want to do the little things for your mate that make him/her feel special? No, it doesn't, and then both people in the relationship may feel unloved and unappreciated. Soon neither is giving to the other or filling each other's needs for love and affection. What do you think happens to intimacy for such a couple? It could become extinct or close to nonexistent. I believe intimacy is the glue that holds a relationship together. It is a continuous expression of love for your partner. You can experience intimacy through many forms in a relationship. You can experience intimacy with each other by just sitting and being comfortable together. You can also share intimacy through touch, a look, a kind word, or a generous gesture. You can experience the physical/sexual act of intimacy through making physical love with each other. It is during this physical bond that you both unite and become one. Sex, if not shared in an intimate way, could just become an act of self-pleasure which is not equal to shared intimacy.

When sharing love and appreciation with your partner, it has to be a give-and-take experience or your bond may fizzle out and die. If only one partner is offering himself/herself in the act of giving and appreciating, he/she will soon get discouraged and may even turn his/her attention to another. It really takes two to stay on top of a relationship and make it harmonious. You must listen to each other and understand each other's needs. If you love someone, you receive by giving. The receiver must acknowledge the giver. If the giving becomes one way and is not returned or acknowledged, the circle is broken. When the bond continues to break over and over again, in time the relationship begins to die. An important thing to remember here is that in order to be a healthy giver and receiver, you must know how to give and receive love yourself.

Imagine a relationship being similar to two trees uniting as one. The two trees by themselves stand firm and strong, and their roots go deep to form a strong foundation. Their leaves are beautiful and their trunks are sturdy through their self-love and self-watering. Their self-love feeds them the nutrients that keep them strong and firm in the ground. When these two trees unite into a partnership, the two become one strong tree. Their branches begin to intertwine with each other and their roots emerge together, growing deep into the ground. Because they know how to water and feed themselves, they are able to water and feed each other nutrients that keep the relationship thriving and strong. Through their own individual strengths, they have created one strong tree that is able to thrive during stormy times.

Now let's look at another scenario. There are two trees barely hanging on by themselves. They don't know how to self-water or self-feed. Their roots are shallow, and many leaves are browned and falling to the ground. They see another tree similar to themselves. They think that if they just attached themselves to this other tree, they could be brighter and grow stronger. They are looking solely to the other tree to feed and water them so they could then be strong and survive. What do you think happens to these two trees as they unite? If they don't know how to feed and water themselves, how then could they give nutrients to another? They don't come from a strong foundation themselves, so what can they give to provide strength and healthy growth in a union? You are right if you see this tree withering and dying. Each tree was unable to provide nutrients for the other, as each was unhealthy and barely hanging on before the two intertwined. If there was a strong tree standing beside a withering tree, do you think the strong and healthy tree would be attracted to the weak and withering tree? No, the strong tree will be drawn to another strong and healthy tree. Be kind to yourself and find your own inner strength. Love yourself and you can then completely love and give to your partner.

Not all relationships are blessed with a healthy circle of giving and receiving. Some relationships may be like the two unhealthy trees just hanging on to survive and unable to give nutrients to the other. Resentment may then build up from frustration that the other isn't making them happy. Soon lack of trust and respect will set in. If you find that this has happened to you and you want to rekindle your relationship, start looking for ways to appreciate your partner more. Begin with appreciating yourself and then pass that appreciation on to your partner. As we've learned before, there was something that attracted you to your mate from the start. There was something you did love about this person or you wouldn't currently be with him/her, would you? If you give love and appreciation out, you will be amazed at the response you will get back. If you start focusing on the positive things about your partner, you will begin to fall in love with him/her all over again, and vice versa. Love will attract love, but criticism will attract only defensiveness, walls, and a breaking of bonds. When you continually focus on the negative aspects of your partner, that's what you will have, a negative experience and a dead or dying relationship. How much more wonderful would it be to focus on your mate's positive attributes? When you start appreciating each other again in a daily fashion, you will bring life and harmony back to your relationship.

Don't forget to stay attractive for each other. I will talk more about this in the "Health and Fitness" chapter. Your own personal upkeep that you maintained when you attracted a mate while you were single should remain with you throughout your partnership. Don't take each other for granted. Stay beautiful/handsome, healthy, and clean, so that when you look in the mirror you find you can appreciate yourself. If you don't maintain a sense of attractiveness, how do you think your mate will perceive you? Keep healthy and fit for yourself and your partner. When you love yourself, you remain lovable. Remember what attracted you to each other in the first place. Love and respect yourself, and in turn your mate will love and respect you. Take time to do little things for your mate to show your love and appreciation for him/her. When you make others feel loved and special, they can't help but return it if they are committed to the relationship.

It is very important to also understand the differences between men and women in a relationship. By the time we have reached adulthood and have been in a few relationships, it should be obvious that men and women are quite different. We are different beings and therefore interpret life from our own inner perspectives. This means that we may interpret the same scenario in a completely different way and we will both be right. Men and women are simply made up of completely different genes, and those are the facts. Once we understand this, it makes things a whole lot easier as we let go of the demand that our mate see and interpret things the same way we do.

Please, women, don't get mad at your man if he doesn't act or react in the exact way you want him to. He simply doesn't understand you and your personal needs. You must communicate this to him, and he still may not understand you, even if he tries. We speak different languages as men and women in a relationship. Understanding each other becomes a tricky road to navigate, but the road becomes a lot smoother if communication is open between both partners.

Women are emotional beings. They love to talk about their feelings and about how their mate might feel. Men don't love this as much. In fact, it may make your man tense and uneasy when you bring up feelings all the time. Understand that men are logical and come from a practical base most of the time. As women, we love to talk, talk, talk, and if feelings are involved, we are even happier.

If a woman is upset, it may just mean that she wants to be listened to. After she expresses her feelings and feels listened to, men should understand that she usually will be ready to move on. If men only knew how many times a woman discusses a certain issue with all of her friends, family, and even passing acquaintances. Women love to bounce situations off as many people as they can and then come up with their own interpretation of the answer. If the woman feels that her man is listening to her and is making a conscious effort to understand her, she will feel better. Usually this is all that it takes for her to move on.

Women want to feel understood and loved. We feel with our emotions. We are sensitive and react with feelings. When we as women feel loved and appreciated by our mates, it makes us want to give love and support back. When women feel loved, they will stand by their men.

Men want to he heard and respected in a relationship. They do not want to feel that their mate is unhappy with them and wants to continuously try to change them. Men want to be loved and accepted for who they are and just want peace in a relationship with a woman. When their woman is happy, they are happy. Pleasing his mate is very important to a man, but he may not understand what his woman wants because he doesn't understand her language. When he thinks he is pleasing her by providing peace and being nonconfrontational, she may be upset because he isn't doing what it is she wants him to. This causes conflict, because his wants and needs may be entirely different from hers. This is where good communication comes in. If good communication doesn't occur here, you can see how conflict can set in, leading to resentments and relationship breakdown.

Communication and compromise are very important ingredients for the survival of a continuous, harmonious relationship. In a marriage or committed relationship, over time there will certainly be some disagreements or differences of opinion. When these come up, communication is very important. I do know that most men hate that dreaded phrase that women love to say, "We need to talk." This phrase is usually like a dagger to a man's heart, and he usually will try to avoid it at all costs. When a woman wants to talk to her man, he usually interprets this as her being unhappy with his behavior in some way. Men want to please their women and make them happy. They don't take it very well when women express concerns about their unhappiness. They immediately try to fix it to make their universe right again. Women want to talk and men want to fix. Each sees it as a way of making things better. How then, you ask, do men and women ever see things eye to eye? Again, I think the key is communication, and understanding and supporting each other's differences.

If men or women play a passive-aggressive game of ignoring their partner when they are upset, and say "nothing is wrong" when questioned, they are only breaking bonds of trust that should exist in a relationship. The relationship needs trust and honesty to survive. There is no room for game playing. Open and honest behavior is what will help the relationship to thrive and survive the storms.

When a woman wants to talk or communicate something to her partner, it is best if the woman begins the conversation in a supportive, nonthreatening way. The conversation could go a lot smoother with less defensiveness if she conveys upfront that she just wants to talk and come to an understanding with her partner. It may not always mean that there is something wrong.

When the couple begins to talk about the issue, it will help if they go into the conversation remembering why they are together in the first place. At the beginning of the conversation, remember that you both love each other and choose to be together. You are there to find a compromise to a situation that has caused some conflict. A compromise can be the solution when two partners meet each other halfway on an issue. Both of you need to drop your defensiveness and blame. Just listen to each other and try to understand the other's point of view. You can agree to disagree and then find common ground to stand together on. Remember, when the discussion is finished, you still love each other and are committed to staying together. Please convey this to each other. This will create safety and security in the relationship. It will relieve the tension and strengthen the trust and bond between you.

It is also very important to communicate your needs to the other. If you get upset at your partner and you haven't communicated what it is you wanted, a miscommunication has occurred and disharmony begins. When you communicate to each other and are heard by the other, harmony flows throughout the relationship.

Finding common ground, communicating, appreciating and supporting each other, as well as sharing intimacy, will carry the relationship through any storm to the other side. It is so important that both partners are in the relationship with both feet and committed to understanding each other's needs. If this does not happen, greener pastures may give the illusion of being more fulfilling and could lure the unfulfilled partner to what he/she thinks is a greener and more exciting ground.

CHEATING, LIES, AND AFFAIRS

I understand that it is in my best interest to feed and cultivate the relationship I am currently in.

I choose to be the best partner I can in my current relationship.

I choose to look for positive attributes in my current partner and remember why I was attracted to him/her in the beginning.

I act with integrity and dignity in all areas of my life.

I am honest with myself and love myself; therefore, I only allow myself to be in healthy relationships with those that treat me with love and respect.

I can speak from experience here that the grass is never greener, and I urge you to nurture and cultivate your own garden. If you venture out believing another can make you happy, you will only find another person's weeds. Remember the beginning of my story as I described my affair with Blake? It was the worst choice I have ever made, and the only positive thing that may come out of it is to try to convince others of the severe consequences if an affair is the direction you are looking towards. Take time to cultivate what you have. Till your own soil and make it rich and healthy. It is from there that your garden will grow strong, healthy, and beautiful. When you get tired of the garden you have created with another in a relationship and think another's garden looks more beautiful, think again.

Stepping out in an affair will only cause you and the many people involved more pain than you can ever imagine. When I stepped out of my first marriage into an affair, I found a roller-coaster ride of emotions and drama beyond my belief. The highs were extremely high, but the lows were so low I barely survived them. This can cause an addictive cycle, because the highs are perceived to be so much more than those found in a normal, healthy relationship. Having experienced this addiction, I will take the normal, healthy relationship any day. It has so much more depth and can actually become much more fulfilling. When properly attended to, a normal relationship with committed, available individuals is real and can be long lasting, while an affair is only an illusion of love and is usually temporary. If you choose to step into an affair with another individual while you or the other is already in a committed relationship, you will fall and may take innocent bystanders down with you. Think hard before you take this step.

If you feel unloved or unappreciated, you can easily justify to yourself the need to be with someone else to get your needs met. I can assure you, those "needs" will only be met temporarily. If you do cheat, lie, or step out into an affair, be prepared for more pain than you have ever experienced in your life. When you put yourself in an extremely unhealthy situation, the world will respond back to you with negative, negative, and more negative. You have to trust me on this one. If you have children involved, think of them. Their little lives will suffer. I encourage you to redirect your selfish energy back to your mate and your family. Reconnect with your current mate and appreciate him or her more. If this doesn't work and the relationship continues to be only one sided in the circle of giving and receiving, you may have to consider taking care of yourself and rethink the relationship. I completely support marriage and committed relationships, but it really takes two to make it work and to create harmony with each other. It takes two to be committed and understand what the other's needs are. If only one is committed to doing what it takes to make it work, he/she may be left feeling unloved and uncared for. If you can relate to this scenario, I suggest you discuss this with your mate in a nonthreatening way and seek professional help to guide you with your decisions.

If you step out into an affair and feel the highest of highs, you may find yourself in a relationship addiction. This happened to me without even knowing or understanding it. I have never been addicted to anything before, nor have I since. Before I knew it, I was hooked, and I would do anything to be with that other person, even if it hurt me and many others. Blake became my drug of choice. When the sadness and pain crept in, I didn't care. I just needed to see him again to get that high so I could temporarily relieve my pain. I did this even if I knew the pain would come back. I felt I had no control. I knew I wanted out of the pain, but I also knew that seeing the man I had the affair with would temporarily ease this painful discomfort. I was lost in the illusion that this was love. I was addicted. I lost myself, my dignity, and all sense of reality. I had no self-love. My desire and need to feed my addiction became more important than anything rational. At the time, I didn't even realize I was addicted. Many suffered because of my selfish need for this high.

I share my story with you to advise those that can relate to it to please think before stepping out into an affair. What do you think it will bring you other than an immediate short-term high? If you are unhappy in your current relationship, having an affair is not the honorable thing to do. It will not replace unhappy with happy in the long run. It is not your answer. It is only an illusion of love. Just know there will be long-term effects and you will cause much pain to yourself and others by involving yourself in an affair. It is not worth it. Find that high in your love for yourself. This is pure love and light that can be found inside of you. It is that part of you that is connected to Spirit. It is so much more fulfilling than any short-term high can be. Seek the light and the light will find you. Seek the darkness and yes, the darkness will surely find you. Remember your choices. Your life is your choice, and I encourage you to seek comfort and safety in purity, light, and love. When you seek darkness, it will give you just that, darkness.

If for some reason your partnership has become an unsafe place for you due to emotional or physical abuse, please take care of yourself and seek refuge from professional institutions that specialize in this area. No one should stay in an abusive situation. You need to be safe and make sure your children, if you have them, are safe. Find the strength to remove yourself from the unsafe environment and get help. This is loving yourself. Seek the light, find your courage, and seek safety. When you seek the light, love will find you. When you step into darkness, remember, darkness will surly meet you there.

ADDICTIONS

I now have the power to be free and love myself.

I make only healthy choices for my life.

I am a whole, healthy being in every area of my life.

I live a life of balance.

I have courage and strength to only seek for myself all that is good and all that is positive.

My definition of an addiction is when you continue to do something you know is harmful for you but you crave it and

ADDICTIONS

can't control the urge to get it because of that "high" feeling, knowing full well that you will come crashing down when the addicted agent is removed. If you continue to do a behavior that you know is harmful to you and you can't easily or don't want to stop it, you are addicted. No matter how you want to rationalize it, you are addicted, and it is your choice to remove the harmful agent from your life so you can create balance and become healthy again.

Addictions come in many forms. One could be addicted to such things as shopping, spending, gambling, overeating, undereating, sex, a relationship, drugs or alcohol, excessive exercise, working; and this list could go on and on. The bottom line is that many get into an addictive situation without ever intending to. They somehow lose themselves to the addictive agent, and before they know it, they feel as if they are unable to live without it. The agent gives them a temporary high that they continue to crave. They give their power away to this agent, many times at any cost. Sometimes the cost could be deadly. Because of their addiction, everything they have loved could be lost, including themselves.

Having been there myself by experiencing a relationship addiction, I do know how hard it is to give up or walk away from an addiction. The suggestion I have for those addicted is to go inside and find your inner strength. Your first strength is in admitting you have an addiction. If you can do this, you have taken your first step towards your recovery. Grow from here. You have given your power away, and it is now time to get it back because your life is your choice. By giving in to your addiction, you are, in a sense, surrendering your power to the addictive agent and allowing it to take control of your life. It is now time to claim your power back. Surround yourself with supportive people, be it your friends or family, and seek out an agency that helps promote recovery from addictions. There are many agencies to help assist you with this. Take steps toward finding your power and freedom again. I do understand that this may not be an easy process but you **must** love yourself through it. It could be a matter of choosing life over death. Even if you remain alive and are still breathing, if you continue to give your power over to your addiction, your disconnection to your emotional and spiritual being may make you feel as if you were dead. You must dig deep, gain control and ask for help. Remember, as you surrender and seek love and light in your life and extend your hand out seeking help, a warm, supportive hand will surely grab you and begin pulling you forward. It is OK to ask for help as you seek your road towards recovery. Pay attention and look for that helping hand. Your true spirit is always there, wanting to reconnect and take you to your place of peace. Trust and believe this.

Once you get your power back, you will be able to walk away from the addicting agent. You will begin to bring balance, peace, and happiness back into your life. You will feel alive again and regain your dignity. You will be found. When you take your life back, you take your power back, and you can begin to live your life the way you intended it. Freedom will be yours again. This is where you can begin to create your dreams into a reality as your life now moves into balance. You can do this. Believe in yourself and grab the hand of those extending their hands to you.

BEING IN BALANCE

I live a life full of balance and wellness.

*I create a balanced life of work, play,
rest, and rejuvenation.*

Because I live in balance, I live in harmony.

When you are living with balance in your life, you are living with peace and harmony every day. Balance comes in physical forms, emotional forms, and a spiritual form. Being in balance may mean something different to each individual. For me, having a balanced life means creating time for the things I have to do, as well as the things I like to do.

We must all eat and sleep each day. Many of us must also work. Some go to school. It is up to each of us to create harmony between our life responsibilities while finding time daily, or weekly, to participate in activities that bring us pleasure, personal fulfillment, and rejuvenation. Eating healthy and finding time to do some form of physical exercise on a routine basis creates physical balance in our bodies. I will go into greater detail on the subject of diet and exercise in the "Health and Fitness" chapter to come. Adequate rest and sleep are also necessary for our bodies to rejuvenate and feel refreshed so we are able to take on other activities in our lives.

Balance also means making time for friends and family. This is part of our emotional balance. Having a support system is important and makes us feel cared for and loved, knowing there is someone else that cares about our well-being. It is also a good feeling to be supportive for another person that you love and care for. It becomes an equal relationship of giving and receiving, offering equal emotional balance. When a relationship is in balance, the circle of giving and receiving is complete. When this happens you know you have been blessed with a loving and caring person in your life that also recognizes the need for balance. Cherish and appreciate this person always.

It is also important to find quiet and down time as well as fun and playful time. Quiet or down time allows us to rejuvenate and refocus. This becomes our spiritual balance. Your body, mind, and spirit need time to refuel. Take some down time each day to reflect on the things that are important to you. Refuel your soul. This can be done in the form of yoga, meditation, or by simply just being quiet while listening to relaxing music. Use this time to reconnect with your inner spirit. Connect with your self-love and your appreciation for all that you have. You could also use this time to visualize your desires. This will create peace for you within your day and remind you who you really are and what is important.

When we are rested, we are then ready to play and have fun. Fun time may be different for each individual. This could be in the form of doing what we are passionate about. We should all understand our passions. When you realize your passion and are able to spend time with it each week, it can offer a lot of fulfillment. Remember to take time for fun in your life. This will prepare you to face other responsibilities that may not be as fun but are still important to accomplish to create balance. The fact that you do follow through on your responsibilities, though, is something to be commended.

If you are out of balance with any of these areas in your life, you may feel it through stress, anxiety, depression, insomnia, anger, and the feeling of being intolerant of many things. This could make you very hard to live with from others' points of view as well as your own. When you are out of balance, you will feel it inside. It can manifest in forms of illness. It is important to understand that you created this lack of balance in your life. There is no one to blame but yourself, and you alone are the only one that can get yourself back into balance. The first step is in realizing it. The second step is to desire more peace and balance in your life. The next and most important step is making different choices and taking different actions to put all the aspects of your life back in balance. When you create more balance, you begin to prioritize what is most important and most valuable to you. If you are in balance, you will take time each day with that which you have given value or priority to.

It may help to make a list of your top priorities and then ask yourself, "Am I giving adequate time to what I have identified as important areas in my life?" If your answer is no, then it may be time to make some changes, creating more balance and giving more energy to those things you value and consider a priority. Again, it's your life, and your choice.

You can look at your life activities through what I call the "balance meter." If you are living one area of your life to an extreme, or spending too much time and energy in one area, then I put you in the red zone on the balance meter. An example of this is someone who is a workaholic. This person might be working fifty or sixty hours a week, or more. This person doesn't have much time for rest, family, general life responsibilities, or play time. Another example is someone spending too much time exercising and not having enough rest time. This can happen to competitive athletes who get caught up in their training, doing it to an excess. I have known athletes like this. They eat, sleep, and talk only "training." Where is the balance in their lives? Their focus is only on taking their bodies to extremes during their workouts. I know this because I have lived it. Your workouts should be enjoyable, not exhausting.

The other end of the meter is the white zone. This is where people spend too much time just doing nothing. They can spend most of the day sitting on the couch watching TV, playing video games, spending hours on the computer, or lying in bed all day. These people are living life with such passivity; life may be passing them by. Their muscles may atrophy due to lack of exercise, and their skin could become pale and dull. Some may have dark circles around their eyes. These people may also have unhealthy eating habits. They rarely see sunshine or feel fresh air. Because they lack interactions with real people, they are at risk of losing their sense of identity. Many of them might suffer from depression. People who live in these extremes are too far into the white zone. They need more balance and life engagement. This could be in the form of just getting out of the house and going for a walk to get fresh air and sunshine. They might even hear some birds singing. I would also recommend some social time with friends or family. Social interactions remind us that we are living creatures. A warm gesture from another helps us remember our sense of identity and self-esteem. When you feel loved and cared for by others, you remember that you are loveable.

The middle of the balance meter is green. This is reserved for people who seem to have mastered a balance in their life between work, play, rest, family responsibilities, friendships, spiritual or reflection time, eating healthy, and a balanced exercise program. Living in the green is where we all should strive to be in order to create peace and harmony in our lives. When we are in balance, we tend to be happier in every area of our lives, and we are able to pass this happy feeling on to others.

Making better choices and changing your actions can change your life to create more peace, harmony, and balance. Having more peace and harmony will create more love for yourself, as you have changed your life to bring yourself more happiness. Congratulations if you have learned to love yourself more by creating a life with balance. You have just become more lovable.

SELF-LOVE

I love myself and only allow situations and people into my life that reflect this back to me.

When I love myself, I am able to give and receive love freely.

Once you have learned to love yourself more, you have found the key to your continuous happiness in life. No one can take it from you. Your love for yourself is found deep inside you, and you get to take it with you wherever you go. There is never a need to feel lonely or alone again. Self-love gives you your power back. Your love for yourself will only allow those into your life that reflect this back to you. Self-love will become your foundation from which you embrace the world. It will give you strength, peace, and continuous joy from within.

Self-love manifests when you take care of yourself in all forms. When you love yourself, you continually put yourself in healthy situations. You take care of your body by eating healthily and exercising regularly. You create time for rest and rejuvenation, thus creating balance in your life. You also protect yourself from harm physically, emotionally, and spiritually as you promote and live a healthy lifestyle. Self-love promotes self confidence, and those around you will easily recognize it.

If you feel you are lacking in self-love and find yourself grasping for it but unable to find it, you may have instead allowed fear or pain to rule your life. It is time for you to make the choice to remove fear from your life and open your heart to love. Self-love comes from deep down inside. As described in earlier chapters, self-love becomes strongest when you are able to find a connection to your inner light, or Spirit, in your heart. Right now, close your eyes and find that connection of love for yourself. Go to your heart center. Only focus on your heart and your love. Remove all other thoughts from your mind. Allow these feelings of love to flow through and around you. They may elicit many emotions within you. So many of us wander through life and feel unlovable. You can change this right now. We are all lovable. I urge you to quiet your mind, go inside yourself, and connect with your heart. You are a beautiful being created on this earth. Forget all of the past. Put it behind a closed door. Today, right now, is a new beginning. You can start a fresh, cleansed, and renewed life this very moment. You don't ever have to live in the past again. All you have is now, and now is the time to give yourself unconditional, everlasting love. It is yours free for the taking. You were born with it. You deserve it. Grasp it, hold it, and embrace it. Open your heart to love and love will find you. Love will change your life. It is your life and your choice to live in fear or to live in love. I urge you to choose love and see how your life can change.

FEAR VERSUS LOVE

I choose to live my life full of love.

I give and receive love easily.

Love surrounds my life in every way.

To live a life full of love is to live with continuous peace and happiness. When you open to receive and give love, it flows easily from and within you. When your heart is open and full of love, you may feel fullness in your chest. We all have felt the intensity of a new love for another. There is an excitement and awareness around us. Everything seems alive. The birds seem to be singing a little louder, the sun warms us more, and all of life just seems to come together easier. Many of us have also experienced a loss of that same love. Soon pain, sorrow, and suffering set in because of that loss. The gift I give to you today is the knowledge that love in your heart can always be with you. No one can take it from you because it is part of you. Love is the answer to create harmony, balance, and unity. Love is unconditional. It is always in our hearts and always there to give and receive. Love is hope. Love is our connection to Spirit. Love is everything beautiful.

The opposite of Love is Fear. Fear is the barrier to pure happiness. Fear blinds the light and destroys hope. Fear creates anxiety and panic and blocks any rational thought. Fear blinds truth. Fear destroys hope. Where love creates balance and harmony, fear creates imbalance and disharmony. Where love creates oneness, fear creates aloneness. Love is unconditional. Fear is all about conditions, justice, and vengeance. Fear is the boulder between you and love. I urge you, if you want peace, happiness, and continuous harmony in your life, remove that bolder of fear that is in your way to unconditional and constant love. Remember, what you focus on, whether it be fear or love, will show up in your life.

To remove this boulder of fear, you can do an exercise in your mind right now. Close your eyes and get comfortable. Visualize yourself on a path. The path can look any way you want, but see yourself on your path towards love and abundance. On that path you see a big boulder. This boulder is in your way of getting where you want to go. You can see beyond the boulder and notice your dreams. There is a beautiful light past the boulder. The boulder represents everything you have created in your life to prevent you from following and living your dream. There may even be many boulders instead of just one. Recognize what these boulders or obstacles are to you. Acknowledge them, thank them for sharing, and then ask them to leave. Be firm. Stand tall and with confidence. Be bold. Speak with conviction. Tell them why you no longer need them in your life. Watch them become weaker, smaller. See your dream life beyond the boulder. In your mind, see yourself easily removing the boulder from your path. You then are able to move easily toward your dreams. See yourself walking down the path you created just for you. Now see yourself arriving at the life you have always dreamed of. Live it in your mind. Smell it, taste it, hear it, touch it, and become it. Just know that after you have removed that boulder that has prevented you from living your life of peace, love, and abundance, you can go to your dream life anytime in your mind. Soon you will dream it into reality.

Fear can represent many things, but it always represents the opposite of love. How would you rather live? Soften your heart and open to receive love. Fear no longer needs to be a part of your life, as it will always prevent you from your true and pure happiness.

ANGER

I always choose understanding, love, and kindness.

I take a time-out when needed and always return to love.

Anger is a product of fear. When we allow the emotion of anger to manifest in us, it can become a very ugly place. People can get hurt through anger. Words can be spoken and actions taken that we may regret later. Fear and anger can make us react irrationally. When we return to love and remember our angry words or actions, they may make us feel embarrassed and ashamed. It is hard to take those words or actions back if they have involved another being. The key is to try to prevent ourselves from ever going to that place of anger.

As I said before, anger comes out of fear. It never ends well. Someone always gets hurt. If you feel yourself moving towards anger, try to stop yourself and look for the real reason provoking this emotion. You may need to take a time-out here before you do or say something you will regret. What is the fear behind this anger? If you acknowledge the fear, thank it for sharing but return your attention towards love. If you do this, you and everyone involved will benefit. Nothing good ever comes out of anger, which sometimes leads to rage or violence. It needs to be stopped before it ever reaches this stage. Because fear blinds light, anger can lead to darkness.

The only good thing that could come from anger is acknowledging the fact that we have moved out of love. It can be a warning sign to us that we are off track and may give us the nudge we need to move back into balance. Pay attention to your emotions. They will always let you know if you've moved off your path to your dream life and away from peace and harmony. When we are on our right path, living a life full of love, our bodies and emotions will feel it. It will produce a life of wellness and we will feel it throughout our whole being. Learn how to move from anger into understanding, love, and forgiveness.

FORGIVENESS

I am easily able to forgive and offer love.

I forgive myself and others from any past hurts.

I now have freedom in forgiveness.

Holding resentment or a grudge towards someone can become part of the boulder or stumbling block preventing peace and harmony in our lives. Holding on to grudges or resentment is another way of holding on to pain. It can weigh very heavily on us and manifest in ways such as illness, insomnia, anxiety, and depression. This grudge becomes a dark spot in our bodies and souls. The key here is to release this resentment and move toward forgiveness. Let the past be the past. All you have is your now and the future you're creating in the present. It is your life and your choice as to how your present and future turn out. By releasing resentment and a grudge towards someone, you will create freedom for yourself.

Blame comes in the same category. Blame can bind us in our own chains. We should never blame someone else for our actions or our situations. We have put ourselves there, and it is our choice to stay or take ourselves out of a bad or unhealthy situation. How we react or respond to a situation is entirely our choice. We can never blame anyone else for our sadness or pain. It is our choice to feel sad, or it is our choice to look for the good and feel happy again. If you look hard, there is always something to be thankful for in every situation. Focus on the good and the positive and you will have more to be thankful for tomorrow. Release the resentment, blame, and grudges and you will find your freedom.

Freedom also comes in forgiveness of self. If you have created a situation from your past that you are not proud of and think you have caused someone else pain or harm, you now have the choice to hold on to that anger and disrespect for yourself or free yourself by asking for the other person's forgiveness, thus creating an avenue to now forgive yourself. If you hold on to that resentment and anger, thinking that you deserve pain because you caused another person pain, please allow yourself to release these unnecessary thoughts. Anger, even if it is towards yourself, is not a healthy emotion to carry around with you. Once you have asked the person you think you have harmed for forgiveness, you are then freed up to create that forgiveness in yourself and offer self-love. Forgiveness and self-love will create purity around you, and you will then be free to give and receive love again. That freedom will bring peace back to your life and a smile back on your face.

I will now give you an exercise you can do to help you release any anger or resentment you have stored up involving yourself or someone from your past. I know this stored-up anger and blame can only lead to sadness and pain in your body, mind, and spirit. It will prevent you from living a life of harmony and love. Remember, insert the name of the person that is the focus of your stored-up anger, be it yourself or others from your past.

Get yourself in a quiet place and a comfortable position. Relax everything in your mind and body as you have done in the previous exercises. You can use peaceful music if that will help. Imagine yourself in a peaceful place in your mind. It is safe there, and you feel comforted and loved. Be in that place until you feel full of peace and love. Now allow that person you hold resentment or anger towards to come in and sit in front of you. You are still loved and safe, and this person cannot hurt you. They are a passive part of this visualization. You can speak to this person and let your feelings out. Try to stay calm and in peace. Tell them what you want to tell them but remember it was always, and still is, your responsibility as to how you react or reacted to them. If they hurt you in any way in the past, just know you are safe now. Feel yourself being safe. Move into your self-love that offers you safety. Now move towards forgiveness. Tell the person you forgive him/her and mean it from your heart. Allow those feelings of anger and hurt to release from your body. You can now ask that person to leave your peaceful place. See yourself removing their negative presence from your life. You are now there alone, still safe, but free of any past resentment. Feel a new feeling of lightness. Your heart can now stay open to allow love back in. This person does not need to be around you anymore. Once you ask the person to leave, release him/her. Don't ask the person back or allow that resentment or blame back into your thoughts. It is now up to you to move on with your life. Let the past stay in the past. Your new life is now balanced, and your body, mind, and spirit are free to receive all that is good. This freedom that you have given yourself will lead to your peace and happiness. It all starts with forgiveness and then moves on to trust.

TRUST

*I live with trust that everything that comes
to me is in my best interest.*

When I trust, I feel free and live in peace.

Trust is a wonderful feeling that allows you to live life with hope. When you trust, you will believe that everything that happens to you is for your best. When you trust those around you, there is a free flow of open energy. To trust is to live without worry. Worry never serves any purpose but to feed our fears. It never resolves any issues. Let go of any kind of worry in your life, as it will manifest in unhealthy ways throughout your body. Worry is only a waste of your time and thoughts and can actually attract that which you are worrying about into your life because you are giving it energy. To live a life of trust is to live a life in close connection to Spirit. Remember, Spirit means something different to each individual, and we should always respect each other's God/Spirit. This is a very personal belief, but when you feel close to your Spirit, you are able to live in trust. Trust is believing that everything will always work out with your best interest. When you want something you do not currently have, trust gives you the peace that if you are meant to have it and it is in your best interest, it will show up in your life. Trust is staying open and allowing yourself to receive. Remember the open/closed door theory? When you trust, you understand that when a door is closed, it is for a purpose. Those who don't trust might try to bang the door open. That is not the best path to take, as they will soon find out. Doors are closed for a reason. If you break them down and plow through them, usually you will find pain and suffering on the other side. If you are smart, you will do a U-turn and eventually find your way back to the beginning, looking for the open door and green light. When you trust and wait, doors open. It is such a wonderful feeling to have patience and trust and then find an open door. When the door is open and the light is green, you feel exhilarated as you pass through. This is when you know you are on the right path and living your "dream life."

Trust starts at an early age. If we learn to trust our environment and the people around us as children, it usually carries over into our adult life. If we experience an unsafe environment, this too will also carry over into our adulthood with mistrust and fear.

A WORD ON PARENTING

*As a parent, I create an environment
of safety and trust for my children.*

*I guide my children through life but also allow them
enough autonomy to evolve into healthy,
responsible adults.*

*I instill self-confidence and self-love in my children by
always making them feel loved and supported.*

When you become a parent, you usually have an overwhelming desire to care for and protect your child. This protective instinct occurs in each species where the parents will actually lay their lives down protecting their young. It is an extremely powerful, instinctual emotion, and most of us would do anything to protect our children. Not everyone is healthy, though, and sometimes the child may experience neglect and abuse because the adult is not in balance. These children may have a hard time even caring for themselves. If they make it past childhood, these children usually grow up with anger, resentment, and many fears. They mostly feel unloved. When you feel unloved, you can build many defenses around yourself to protect yourself. You may want to keep the world out, and many build defenses such as withdrawal, depression, addictions, obesity, anger, abuse of others, or creating clutter and chaos around their lives. This child can grow up to be unmotivated to succeed as an adult. Because they have felt unloved as children, they don't believe in themselves.

One problem currently facing children today is their newfound escape into the video age and the world of cyberspace. If they spend too much time there, they lose perspective on what reality is. Their world is their computer, and they are on it continuously throughout the day and into the night. Interpersonal relations with actual people become few and far between, as they have established unreal relationships with someone on the other end of the computer screen. This world is an illusion but seems safe to those who feel they are less than those that participate in the real world. It can become an addiction, and other responsibilities in their life may suffer. Because it is a world of illusion and cannot touch or give back, many kids sink into depression as they have a hard time engaging and living in the real world again. They lose their social skills, and many lose their self-image.

It is our job as a parent to create a safe environment and promote self-worth in our children. It is also our job to guide them and help them find balance. This does not mean doing everything for them. Many young adults are still completely dependent on their parents because their parents have created this dependency. It is also our job as a parent to let our kids go in a gradual, healthy way as they are growing up. They need guidance, but they also need to learn responsibility as they are growing into adulthood. If we continue to enable our kids, they will never find themselves as adults. "Spoiled" is the word that comes to mind instead of a healthy, whole individual. We are doing our children a disservice by doing everything for them. It is important to encourage them, support them, and guide them into helping themselves.

Creating a healthy environment for our children as they are growing up is a balance between providing a loving, healthy atmosphere where they feel cared for and safe as well as allowing them the freedom to feel autonomous and learn responsibilities. Creating a positive and loving environment is the best role model we can give to our kids. Their home environment forms the foundation for the rest of their lives, and it is where they learn how to react to life events. By being positive with your children and teaching them that they can succeed in anything they desire, you are giving them a gift that will allow them to follow their dreams. If their home foundation does not feel safe and they are taught that they can't succeed, they will grow up with fears that will hold them back and block them from their full potentials. Their poor self-image can reflect what they create and have in their life. If they believe in themselves because you believed in them, they will use this to move mountains. On the other hand, if they were taught that life is a struggle and were told they were worthless, what do you think they will create in their lives? You are right if you are thinking lack of motivation and imbalance. Many will remain stagnant for fear of moving forward.

While growing up, my mother gave my three sisters and me the gift of continuously boosting our self-esteem and self-image. She was always behind us, telling us we could be or do anything, and she loved to boast to anyone that would listen about how wonderful we were. She continues to do this to this day. At age eighty-eight, we are still her babies and she would do anything for us. She has been the motivating force behind each of our successes. It is because of her that I believe I can conquer anything I set out to do. I have tried to continue the pattern and instill this in my own children. It is not always easy, but I have learned to stay the course and keep my eye on my dream. If you do this, your dream will be your reality. I encourage you to share your children's dreams with them, support them, and instill self-confidence and self-esteem early on. Then sit back and watch them blossom.

SELF-IMAGE/EATING HABITS

I love myself and understand that I have created every-thing I see when I look in the mirror.

When I look in the mirror, I am pleased with what I see.

I love myself inside and out and make healthy choices that mirror this love back to me.

Ask yourself right now, "How is my image of myself?" How do you see yourself on the outside? As you are starting to understand now, you have created everything that is in your life by your choices, thoughts, and actions. When you look in the mirror, what you see is also what you have created. How you look on the outside reflects how you feel about yourself on the inside. If you love yourself, it will show in how you care for yourself through your outward appearance. Ask yourself right now, "Do I like what I see when I look in the mirror? When I look at my face, does it look sad, tired, and worried? How do my eyes look? Do they look open and alive, or do they look puffy, sad, and worrisome? How does my hair look? How does my face look? How do I wear my clothes? Am I happy with my body? Do I carry more weight than my body needs? Am I thinner than I should be?" You have created everything you see when you look in the mirror. If there is something you don't like, you have the power to change it, or change the way you think about it. If there is something in your appearance that is permanent or unchangeable, accept it and allow it to be part of you. Embrace yourself as you are. By accepting that part of yourself that is a natural occurrence, you are loving yourself completely. As you completely accept and love yourself, you will see a total change in your outer appearance. Your whole outward being will reflect the love and balance you have created from within. You will have a healthy glow about you, and others will notice you as beautiful and lovable. When you love yourself, you will care for and love your body.

The natural effects of aging do not apply here. As we age, our body and face change. If we are happy and content with ourselves and our lives, we can embrace the aging process with grace and dignity. Aging is natural and will happen to each of us. Many try to fight this, but I do believe we can be beautiful or handsome at each stage of our lives. When you are happy and feel love, it will show up as a natural glow around you. Many will feel this from you and want to be near you. You will exude a self-confidence because you have inner love and inner peace. It comes from the inside out. This natural glow stays with you throughout each stage of life, and you will always look beautiful or handsome to yourself and others. On the other hand, if you do not love yourself, it also shows up in your outer appearance. Your stress, worries, and fears will be apparent just by looking at you. Stress and worry can cause excess wrinkles on your face, show up in your eyes, and change your posture or the way you carry yourself.

EATING HABBITS

I eat foods that my body needs for fuel and am able to balance the caloric intake for my body to be healthy and strong.

I eat fun foods in small quantities with a healthy balance of good foods.

*I eat until I'm full and then stop,
understanding my body's needs.*

*I eat plenty of foods that are healthy for me,
such as fresh fruits, vegetables, and lean protein.*

I have healthy eating habits.

There are many other things we can do to ourselves that will affect our outer appearance. Everything you eat, drink, and do to your outer body reflects how you look. When you love yourself, you will care for your body, but many people today abuse their bodies. If you live in an industrial society, food is usually readily available. Fast food makes food quick and easy to get. Many times food becomes a social event, and people keep eating and eating and eating way past the point of being full. Cars and public transportation have made it easy to get from one place to another. We can passively sit as we go from point A to point B to retrieve food. In days of the past, and in rural societies, humans had to hunt and work for food. Food was a means of survival and was eaten as a form of fuel for their bodies to continue to exist. There was no form of transportation other than their feet, and exercise became part of their daily existence. In more advanced societies, food is easy to come by and is abundant in stores and restaurants. You don't even have to lift a finger to make it because it can also be delivered to your door. As you can guess where I'm going with this, many of us have become lazy, and food may no longer be used as a source of survival. Food often gets consumed as a form of enjoyment or as a social event, many times past the point of hunger. Food can also be used as a form of comfort or as a means of filling a void within.

Excess eating can become an addiction which, as we all know now, leads to unhappiness and a feeling of low self-worth. We have learned from previous chapters that addictions cause us to give our power away to that which we are addicted to. In a food addiction, the high comes from hand to mouth to chewing and then swallowing. That is the end of it. It is no more than the short time it takes to eat and swallow the food. That is the end of the high. After that, comes the feeling of being overstuffed. Shame from uncontrolled behavior may also set in. Thus the feeling of unworthiness and being unlovable may come. The vicious cycle continues as we reach for more food to try to comfort or fulfill us. Food is only a temporary fulfillment, though.

Food, after it is eaten, turns to fuel in our bodies in the form of glucose and, if not used, gets stored as excess fat. As you can see, if you eat more food than your body needs to function in its daily routine, it all gets stored as fat because it is in excess to what your body needs. I will talk more on this in the "Health and Fitness" segment.

Think about what you put in your mouth. The saying "you are what you eat" sounds cliché but is actually very true. It has become common knowledge that eating fresh foods with plenty of fruits and vegetables is very good for our bodies. It is also well known that fried foods, fast foods, and foods high in saturated or trans fats are not. We all know which foods aren't good for us; for example, cheeseburgers, fries, milkshakes, pizza, all fried foods, most fast foods, and most of the desserts. These may be fun foods but not at all healthy to eat. If eaten in excess, they *will* add extra fat to your body.

Foods high in fat can produce many health risks, such as heart disease and stroke. Excess fat can create plaque, which lodges on the walls of your arteries. This is what causes heart attacks and strokes, because the plaque will reduce the opening of the artery and restrict blood flow which carries oxygen to the cells. To our human bodies, oxygen means life. It is what keeps our cells alive. It is what keeps us alive.

Obesity can also cause many other health risks, such as hypertension (high blood pressure) and type II diabetes. Each gram of fat is twice as many calories compared to carbohydrates and protein. Research has also shown that foods high in fat can increase the risk of cancer. Being aware of what we eat is imperative to an overall healthy and happy life.

Smoking cigarettes is another form of abuse many do to their bodies. I could go on and on about the health risks associated with smoking, but because we are talking about self-image, I want to limit our discussion to how smoking affects your outer appearance. Smoking dehydrates and deprives the skin of oxygen and can increase the signs of aging on your face. There is actually a term for this called "smoker's face." Lines and wrinkles become more apparent as smoking depletes the collagen in a smoker's skin. His/her face looks greyer. Discoloration of the teeth occurs from the stain caused by nicotine. Nicotine can also promote hair loss. As you visualize this in your mind, it is not a pretty sight. This may sound harsh, but I want to hit this point hard. This is Your Body and Your Choice. You have been given this one body to treat kindly.

Excess alcohol is another form of abuse people can subject themselves to that harms them emotionally as well as physically. Alcohol affects circulation by expanding the blood vessels. This causes thread veins, often on the face, and can produce a purple "drinker's nose" if an excess is consumed. A reddened face with puffy eyes is also a side effect. Alcohol is usually high in calories, such as with beer. If you are watching your caloric intake, you should make every calorie count as fuel for your body. Again, I will not go on and on about the many adverse effects of excess alcohol, but instead speak only of what it does to your outward appearance for the purpose of staying on point. If you want to learn more about this subject, simply Google "alcohol abuse." Volumes have been written about the detrimental effects alcohol abuse can cause to your whole being and to those around you. If this is a problem for you, I urge you to seek help and regain control of your life. Find the self-love that is abundant for you if you just seek it.

There are many other actions or choices we can make externally to create our outward appearance. Examples include excess sun exposure, body tattoos, body piercing, how we dress, how we wear our hair, our cleanliness, etc. Just know that what you see when you look in the mirror is what you have created. You have the power to change anything about yourself. Love yourself, love your body, and just believe that you are a beautiful being who deserves love. The beauty in your outer appearance will follow. It is your body, and your choice.

HEALTH AND FITNESS

My body is healthy and strong, and I incorporate a regular exercise program into my life.

I am able to create myself as a whole and healthy being, physically, emotionally, and spiritually.

I eat foods that are healthy and good for me.

I love myself as a healthy and fit being.

I have been passionate about wellness and have been working in the health and fitness industry for most of my life. I am currently a registered nurse as well as an American Council on Exercise certified personal trainer. After working as a nurse in open heart surgery for over twenty-five years, I have witnessed the end result of improper care for one's body. I have seen many that are hanging onto life by a thread due to their creation of imbalance and inadequate diet and exercise in their lives. It is now my passion to teach preventative health in creating a balanced and happy existence. As stated before, health in our body, mind, and soul is free to each of us. It is our choice to partake in it. The following are simple guidelines to reach this goal of a healthy body.

DIET

Food is a big topic. It has different meanings for each of us. What many tend to forget is that food was meant to fuel our bodies instead of indulge them. The key is to eat sensibly. It can be stated very simply that a healthy diet should balance the number of calories you eat with the number of calories you burn. A healthy diet also includes eating more fresh foods and less fried, frozen, or prepared foods. Our diets should include plenty of fresh fruits and vegetables, whole grains, and foods high in fiber. Dairy produce can be fat free or low in fat. Meats should be lean, such as fish and the white meat of poultry. Dark poultry meat has more fat than white meat. It is important to drink plenty of fluids but limit beverages and foods high in sugars. You can also reduce your salt intake by eating more fresh foods and not adding salt. If you are used to a lot of salt, I would suggest that this has only become a habit for you. If you stop salting your food, after a time you will not notice it. Foods high in sodium and foods with added salt, such as pretzels and highly salted popcorn, will no longer taste good to you. To make healthier choices, you may have to break old habits. Instead of fried chips, try baked. They offer less fat. Soft spreads are a better nutritional choice than butter. One tablespoon of butter has seven grams of fat and thirty milligrams of cholesterol, as opposed to a soft spread with only two grams or less of fat and no cholesterol.

The American Heart Association recommends that your total fat intake for the day should be less than 35 percent of your total calories. Saturated fat should be less than 7 percent, trans fat less than 1 percent, and cholesterol should be less than three hundred milligrams per day. Saturated fat is the main dietary cause of high blood cholesterol. Saturated fat is found mostly in foods from animals and some plants. The animal fats include beef, veal, lamb, pork, dark poultry meat, butter, cream, milk, cheeses, and other dairy products made from whole and 2 percent milk. These animal-fat foods are all high in cholesterol. The plant fats include coconut oil, palm oil, and cocoa butter.

Trans fats are another fat that increases health risks. Trans fat is a fat created in an industrial process that adds hydrogen to liquid vegetable oils to make them more solid. Many companies use trans fats in their foods because they make those foods easier to use, inexpensive to produce, and longer lasting. These fats are used by many restaurants and fast food chains to deep fry foods. These oils can be used many times in commercial fryers, thus creating an ease in mass production. Trans fats also give foods a desirable taste and texture. Foods high in trans fats are mostly fried foods, such as french fries, doughnuts, baked goods, pastries, pizza dough, pie crusts, cookies, and some crackers. If you look on labels, trans fat is also referred to as "partially hydrogenated oils." Pay attention to what you eat. Your body deserves it.

The American Heart Association recommends limiting the amount of trans fat you eat to less than 1 percent of your daily calories. That means if you need a daily caloric intake of two thousand calories, no more than twenty of those calories should come from trans fats. That small number makes a big statement and may be an eye opener to many. To summarize, the saturated fats and trans fats can increase our body's bad cholesterol, LDL, as well as decrease the good cholesterol, HDL. The good fats are the polyunsaturated and monounsaturated fats found in fish, nuts, seeds, avocados, soybeans, and olives. These fats can actually help in lowering our body's bad cholesterol, LDL. These fats should only be eaten in moderation, though, as with everything we do in life. A healthy choice would be to keep these fat calories to 25 percent to 35 percent of our daily caloric intake.

Junk food is fun food for some but has little nutritional value. These foods may be fun to eat and provide instant energy but can produce many unhealthy results if eaten in excess as described above. The United States Department of Agriculture (USDA) revised the Food Pyramid in the 1990s to recommend a good balance of foods to eat daily. I am sure many of you have heard of the USDA Food Pyramid. Just for fun and for a small review, I will include a summary of the recommendations. You can compare it to what your daily diet consists of. Fats, oils, and sweets have no daily recommendations, and it is advised that we eat them in low quantities. In the dairy or milk, yogurt, and cheese group, it is recommended to eat two to three servings of one to two ounces per day. In the protein or meat, poultry, fish, beans, eggs, and nuts group, it is recommended to eat two to three servings of two to three ounces per day. In the vegetable group, the USDA recommends three to five servings daily. The fruit group is two to four daily servings. The grains group includes bread, cereal, rice, and pasta and is the biggest daily recommendation with six to eleven servings a day. Over the decades, grains have become the largest component in some diets. Meats and dairy have decreased their role in a healthy lifestyle.

Many by now have heard of the terms "free radicals" and "antioxidants." Do we all actually know what this means? I will try to break it down in easy-to-understand terms. Free radicals occur in our bodies as a by-product of abnormal oxidation in some molecules. These molecules then become abnormal, leaving the molecule weak and unstable. This can cause a chain reaction that can cause cell damage. Free radicals can also be introduced into the body through the environment from such things as pollution, radiation and x-rays, cigarette smoke, and herbicides. When these free radicals are formed, they can result in the disruption of our living cells and play a role in health conditions including the aging process, cancer, and arteriosclerosis (plaque in the arteries).

Normally the body can rid itself of most free radicals because antioxidants from fruits and vegetables that we consume are high in vitamins such as C and E. These antioxidants will terminate these abnormal chain reactions and remove the free radicals. Fruits and vegetables have become increasingly popular because of the high content of antioxidants they contain. They should become a part of our daily food intake.

EXERCISE

DREAM BIG
TAKE RISKS
ACCEPT LOSS
BUT NEVER GIVE UP
AND YOU WILL ARRIVE

A normal, healthy lifestyle cannot be limited to a healthy diet alone. Exercise plays an important part in creating a balance of health and fitness. There are many benefits to a regular, balanced exercise program. One big benefit is it helps combat many health risks such as heart disease, obesity, type 2 diabetes, hypertension, stroke, and osteoporosis. Exercise also produces endorphins, which make you feel good. A balanced exercise program could improve your overall mood and self-esteem because you have a sense of accomplishment and pride when you are finished working out. You also feel good because you know you are doing something positive to create a strong and healthy body. Exercise can also help you sleep better. Your heart and lungs are strengthened, and there is increased oxygen and nutrients for your tissues. All of this is common knowledge, so you may ask, "Why don't more people exercise?" You may even ask this question about yourself. Let's look into it further.

Exercise is an excellent way to manage your weight. The more intensely you exercise, the more calories you burn. It is then concluded that if you want to lose weight, you have to burn more calories than you consume. This seems like a very simple and logical statement, but why then are there so many overweight and obese people in the world? Obesity has become an epidemic on an international scale. The statistics are staggering, with millions of overweight, obese, and morbidly obese people in this country alone. Because of increased westernization in other countries, including developing countries, the diet of fast foods and junk foods has become a worldwide obsession. This overweight problem has also filtered down to our children. Obesity in children has now become an epidemic internationally as well.

OK, enough with the overwhelming discussion of diets and foods. The big question here is, what can we, or better yet you, do to fix this in your personal life? I would first say, let's get back to the basics of why I have written this book. I truly believe the key to happiness and creating a healthy lifestyle is derived from pure self-love. I have been drilling "healthy diet and lifestyle" into you, and it may be hitting home for some of you. You may feel yourself squirming, as you may not yet have a good handle on how to create this in your life. Hang on, because we can get through this. Just keep an open mind and an open heart. At this point, take a deep breath, wrap your arms around yourself, and just offer that unconditional love that is available to each of you in a continuous, everlasting flow. Know there is always hope. Believe in yourself and believe in your dreams. After you feel centered, let's move on to the topic of a healthy, balanced exercise program that you can easily incorporate into your life. A healthy exercise program will be easy for you, because you desire a balanced, healthy life. As you love your body, you will care for it more.

There are three forms of exercise to incorporate that create a healthy, balanced program. The first is, of course, cardiovascular or aerobic exercise. This exercise is the key to weight loss and/or maintaining one's weight throughout one's life. It also works the most important muscle in your body, your heart. As your heart gets stronger, it can deliver more oxygen to your cells, which makes for a healthy, happy body. Cardio/aerobic exercise is all about the heart rate. You have a resting heart rate and you have a working heart rate. It is the working/exercising heart rate that determines how many calories you are burning during an aerobic exercise routine, as well as the intensity of your workout. As your heart beats faster (in a controlled exercise setting) and your muscles contract from movement, your body needs to burn more fuel (glucose) to keep up with the demand. When weight loss is your objective, make sure you are burning more fuel (calories) than you are putting into your body.

We each have individual fitness levels and risk factors, so we all should start working out according to our own personal needs. If you are a novice, start out slow. I would advise you to consult your personal physician before starting any exercise program. If he/she has given you the green light, I would then advise you to get a personal trainer to help you get started and stay safe. A trainer can guide you in your workout routines and let you know a desired heart rate that coincides with your condition and your desired results. If your physician has given you the OK to get started in a normal exercise program, it is a rule of thumb to try to maintain a heart rate of at least 70 percent of your heart rate maximum for thirty to forty-five minutes, three to four times per week. Your trainer can let you know what your exercise heart rate should be according to your fitness level. If you can't afford a trainer, you can calculate this yourself. In the morning before you get up, take your resting heart rate for one minute. The formula is 220 minus your age minus your RHR (resting heart rate). To get your heart rate percentage of your maximum HR, take the remaining number and multiply it by .60. Then add your RHR to this number. This will give you your workout heart rate at 60 percent of your heart rate max. You can do the same for 70 percent, 80 percent, and 90 percent. OK, you see the personal trainer coming out in me. I will try to break this down a little more for you. Let me give you an example of how to calculate your desired exercise heart rate. After you determine your own resting heart rate (RHR) by taking it for one minute when you first wake up, just insert your own age and RHR in the required areas below. For the example below, I used an age of 50 with an average RHR of 70 beats per minute.

220 - 50 (age) = 170 – 70 (RHR) = 100
100 x .60 = 60 + 70 (RHR) = 130 (60% max HR)
100 x .70 = 70 + 70 = 140 (70% max HR)
100 x .80 = 80 + 70= 150 (80% max HR)
100 x .90 = 90 + 70 = 160 (90% max HR)

An average workout would be to maintain a heart rate of 70 percent of your maximum heart rate for at least thirty minutes. If you used the above formula, that would be a heart rate of about 140. If you are just starting out you may want to work up to this. You can work out at 60 percent of your heart rate max for as little as fifteen to twenty minutes to start with. Each workout depends on each individual's fitness level. This is why it is important to get approval from your physician and seek the guidance of a personal trainer. This is important if you have never worked out or if it has been quite a while since you have been involved in a regular exercise program. When you are ready, if you want to increase your workout to become stronger or simply to lose weight, take your heart rate up to 80 percent of your maximum heart rate for as long as you can. If using the above formula, that number would be 150 beats per minute. The longer you can keep your heart rate high and still feel fairly comfortable, the better the results if you are trying to lose weight. I would recommend going up to 90 percent of your maximum heart rate only if you are doing interval training. Interval training is taking your heart rate to a maximum level for a short period of time and then dropping it back down to give yourself a rest. In interval training, you would continue this pattern for a given amount of time, increasing and decreasing your heart rate in intervals. This will help increase your heart muscle strength and overall fitness level. Please be advised to do this and any form of exercise only after your doctor has given you permission. Interval training should be done by those not novice to exercise. Increasing your heart rate will increase your caloric expenditure. If weight loss is your objective, this will help you burn more calories than you take in. It is important to remember, proper diet needs to accompany a regular exercise regime to have adequate results.

Strength training is a second form of exercise that creates a balanced and healthy body. Strength training is predominantly weight training, which tones and shapes your muscles. Strength training is important because it makes us stronger in our daily activities. It also helps slow the aging process, because as we age, our muscles tend to get smaller if they are not used. This results in decreased mobility. Strength training combined with aerobic exercise makes you generally feel better about yourself. It makes you feel stronger, in more control of your body, and helps you to stay active throughout your life. Strength training is simply training with weights. If you are intimidated by the gym scene, a personal trainer can help you with simple weight training exercises to get you on your way. In strength training, the body muscle parts are broken down into groups. These muscle groups include your arms, such as biceps/triceps, your chest, your shoulders, your back, your legs, and your abdominals. In working each of these muscle groups, you are creating a balanced, toned body.

Flexibility training is the final form of exercise that gives you a complete and balanced workout. This form of exercise is for your muscles and joints. Through proper stretching, your muscles and joints will stay flexible, bend easily, and prevent injuries such as muscle strains or sprains as well as tendon inflammation due to overuse and inflexible joints. Yoga has become very popular and is a good way to increase your flexibility. You can also stretch on your own. Just remember to stretch when your body and muscles are warmed up and to hold your stretch for a least a minute, elongating the muscles into the stretch. A rapid bouncing motion is not recommended here, as it could actually cause damage to your joints and muscles. The key is to hold your stretch as long as possible, take a break, stretch another muscle, and return to the previous muscle as you hold the stretch again. In being flexible, you will enhance your overall fitness and performance.

One last note on fitness is the topic of overtraining. I have experienced this during my triathlon and marathon training days. I definitely promote endurance exercise, but it must all be done with balance. When you get into longer exercise routines and endurance training, the tendency to overdo it becomes an increasing problem. You have to ask yourself, "Where is the balance here?" I strongly promote having goals and dreaming big. Dreaming big may be completing an Ironman triathlon. This is a 2.5-mile swim, 112-mile bike ride, and a 26.2-mile run all in one race. I'm sure the completion of such a grueling race is an exhilarating experience, but as you can imagine, the training for this is excessive. I commend those that dream this and actually complete it. Training for a marathon also takes a lot of time and commitment. I have completed eight marathons, including the Boston, and have experienced a life of training that was not in the best balance. Completing this goal of running a marathon is a wonderful feeling of accomplishment, and I also applaud all those that have dreamed it and made it a reality. I just urge you all to remember that balance in every aspect of your life will lead to purity and true body, mind, and soul connection.

Health and fitness have become quite extensive topics here, as they have always been big passions of mine. Without a healthy body, how can your inner self be at peace? It is one big package. As you become more gentle and loving to your inner being, your desire to create a healthier outer being will prevail. You are now beginning to create a complete package of wellness in your mind, body, and soul. We are not finished yet, though. Creating balanced and healthy patterns in your life may mean you need to change or undo unhealthy patterns that continue to repeat in your life.

REPEATING PATTERNS

*In my life I am able to learn from my past
and now make healthy choices.*

I have a life full of balance, peace, and harmony.

I only attract that which is healthy and positive to me.

*I am a whole, healthy individual and
live a life full of abundance.*

As you travel on your journey through life, you want to
have a clear path leading you towards inner peace and
happiness. The goal is to have continuous, positive energy

propelling you forward towards your dreams and to be able to live in your dream life throughout your journey. To reach a dream life, one must understand that to live and breathe is to learn and grow. As challenges come forth in our life, our growth to new levels of inner peace and happiness depends on how we handle or react to these challenges. If you don't learn and you don't grow, you may find yourself in a rut, stuck in and/or repeating patterns.

Ah yes, repeating patterns. This would be a good time to take a closer look at your life and notice if the same life situations or challenges continue to show up for you. In other words, do similar situations continuously happen to you over and over again? This could be a different scene with different actors, but the same outcome happens in your life, over and over again. Examples of this are such sayings as:

- Every time I try to lose weight, I just gain it right back.
- I never seem to have enough money.
- My relationships never turn out well.
- Men always leave me.
- Women are always mean to me.
- I always attract a controlling partner.
- I can never hold down a steady job.
- I am always getting sick.

Do you identify with any of these scenarios? Because we have created a certain "story" about ourselves by the time we become adults, what we believe about our story is actually what continues to play out in our lives. People who see themselves as being overweight and believe this story will continue to be overweight. If they change their story to believing they are thinner, with a healthy and stronger body, and continue to see and believe this, they will change their actions and patterns in life to create their new story. People who believe they never have enough money can change this by changing their story to believing and seeing that they always have more than enough money to have everything they want. By changing this scarcity story to one of abundance, their actions and patterns will change and they will begin to now attract abundance and always have more money than they need.

Those who have had continuous failed relationships are able to change their story, too. Depending on what they've been attracting in the past, they can change their story to say that "I only have emotionally, physically, and spiritually available people in my life." You can take this a step further by saying, "I have a wonderful, loving relationship with my partner, and we have a perfect balance of giving and receiving. We live our lives together, full of love, respect, appreciation, acceptance, and harmony."

If you are someone who has always believed that you live with illness, or frequently get sick, I am sure that's what you have in your life. Start seeing yourself with a whole and healthy body. Start saying and believing, "My body is healthy and strong." As you keep telling yourself this new story, you may find yourself eating better and exercising more. Soon you may find yourself free of illness as you bring more health and fitness into your life. Your new thoughts will attract to you new choices and a new reality that matches your new story. As you start loving yourself again, your life will reflect this.

You can change your repeating patterns by changing your story. If you have come to an end of a certain chapter in your life which seems to have been a continuous, repeating life scenario for you, you now have two choices. One choice is to continue on your same path and look for something or someone to replace this empty feeling you have. If you do this, you will more than likely continue to repeat the pattern with the same outcome because you have not changed yourself, your path, or your story. Another choice is to take a time out, reflect on the pattern you've continued to attract, and decide you want to make a change. Making a change from old, habitual behaviors always takes courage. This change usually comes at a point in your life when you say to yourself, "No more," "Enough is enough," or "Never again." Through these words you can derive strength.

You will receive strength to change because continuing on with the same results has now become unacceptable to you. I love the saying, "If you always do what you've always done, you will always get what you've always gotten." This is a very powerful statement, and very true. Think it over as you look at your life. What is it that you have always gotten from what you have always done? If you are unsatisfied with what you have always gotten, now is the time to make the change in what you've always done to receive a new outcome. It is Your Life and Your Choice. You can now make the change by changing your story.

CHANGING YOUR STORY

I now tell a story of abundance and have abundance in my life in every way.

My story reflects one of health and fitness, and my life has responded with a healthy and fit body.

My story now tells of having loving, harmonious relationships in my life, and my life reflects this back to me.

When you find yourself repeating the same patterns over and over again, it can feel as if you are in a dryer going round and round, unable to find your way out. I have felt this before until I finally had to say "*Stop, I want out.*" This is the point when you take your power back. You find your voice when you say, "No more!"

As I said before, it takes a lot of strength and courage to change a habitual behavior that isn't producing the outcome you desire. You may not even understand what that behavior is, but you do see the same outcome showing up in your life over and over again. The power comes from deciding to make the change. The strength comes from having had enough and refusing to accept this outcome anymore. Just know you are not alone. As I described in the chapter "Connection with Spirit," we now understand that we are all an extension of Spirit. We are all connected in some way. Though you may not feel love from everyone, just know that they are all living their own stories, and how they react to you is not always about you but about what they are learning and manifesting through their own individual stories. I support you in wanting to make a change to move towards your dream life and creating peace and harmony around you. I did it, and now you can. In your mind, take my hand, as I extend it out to you. We can do this together. Love yourself and the world will reflect this back to you.

When I decided enough was enough, I knew I had to take a time-out and change myself to change what I was attracting. I had to change certain habitual patterns and thoughts to create more love around me. You can also do this as you choose a new, healthy life yourself.

When you take a time-out, it does not mean that you stop life all together. You have to continue on with your responsibilities, such as work, school, and family. Keeping loving and supportive friends and family around you at this time is also important. A time-out simply means you do just that. Take some "me" time to do the things that make you happy. Pamper yourself in healthy ways. Take time to reflect on things in your life that haven't worked and then let them go. Start eating healthier and exercising more. There is no doubt this will make you feel better about yourself. Now is the time to only reflect on the things you do want in your life and remove those that no longer serve you. Take some quiet time to think this through. What is it that really makes you happy and that has long-lasting fulfillment? What are your goals and dreams? I want you to just focus on your goals and dreams as you continue in your daily routines. Take time out each day to visualize your dream life, and also be thankful for everything you currently have in your life that makes you feel happy and feel safe. The more you are thankful for all that you have today will bring more to be thankful for tomorrow. Only focus on what you are thankful for and what you want instead of what you don't have or what you lack. Remember, what you focus your attention on will show up in your life. This change in your thoughts is changing your story. Be good to yourself. Use the quiet time to continue to feel and visualize love and peace around you. Reach your hand out and love will find you. As you change your story and slowly start to engage more with life's interactions, you will find that your old ways don't work for you anymore because they are not part of your new story. Stay focused on your new story, goals, and desires. Take them with you always. When you have a moment during your day, reflect on them. Think of your dream life and your appreciation for all that is around you before you go to sleep each night and in the morning when you awake. Make your new vision for yourself a part of your everyday thoughts, and soon you will be living your dream life because your actions and choices will reflect your new thoughts and desires. You will attract those desires to you. If you find yourself doing an old habitual behavior from your past that created undesirable outcomes, you will find yourself feeling tight, anxious, unable to sleep, and unhappy.

These are your emotions telling you your behavior is not aligned with your new story. Pay attention to how you feel. When you feel light and happy, you know you are on the right path. When you feel tense and anxious, you know you can change your thoughts and actions to get back on your path leading to your dream life. When you do this, you will start to feel happy and light again. When you change your story, you will see your dreams arrive in your reality.

HAVING A DREAM

As I dream and envision what I want my reality to be,
my future reality becomes my dream.

When I envision my dream life, I feel happy and elated.

As I dream, I am creating my future.

When I dream, I dream big, because I realize I
can be and do anything I dream of.

If you don't have a dream, you don't have a direction. Without a direction, you are stuck and stagnant. Your life will move at a slow pace and without intent. You then allow yourself to be vulnerable to other people's intentions. This could put you in unhappy situations, or even throw you into someone else's story or chaos. Be clear on your direction, dreams, goals, and desires.

Having a dream, goals, and desires gives you a reason to rise out of bed each morning. It gives you a purpose to go on and fulfillment when you achieve momentum towards that dream or goal. It is very rewarding to have a goal and achieve it. You always hear successful people say, "Dream big, go for it, because you can do anything you set your mind to." We are the masters of our own destiny. The only limitations we have in life are the limitations we put on ourselves. Look at the gold medal Olympic athletes. They are regular people just like you and I but they had a dream. They followed their dreams, and with hard work and determination they reached unreachable goals. Michael Phelps did this when he won his eight gold medals in swimming at the 2008 Summer Olympics in Beijing. The whole world stood by in awe. Each time he came out for a race, he was focused and did not make eye contact with anyone. He would listen to his music and visualize the end result he wanted for the race. Many successful athletes visualize their results before a competition. They visualize themselves strong during the event and actually winning it. This comes true for many who are able to keep their focus on their desired end results and remove any fear or doubts they might have about being strong.

On another note, who would have thought we would ever have a black president in this country? President Obama went against all odds, visualized his dreams, and pursued them, though many doubted him. He forged through adversity and attacks from the opposing party. He stayed focused, stayed the course, stayed true to himself, and became victorious. His inauguration in January 2009 was a memorable moment for this country and for the world. Through his dreams of creating a better country and a better world, many people now share his dream and are working to give back to this world and those in need.

Adam Lambert, an international rock star, also had a dream. He spent many years singing and performing in different venues. Many of them did not allow him to express his true self. He was born with an amazing gift, his voice. He had a dream of sharing this gift with many and of being a rock star who performed before the world. Because of his dream, he was led to try out for *American Idol* in the fall of 2008. Much to his surprise, because he felt he was different and a little edgy from the normal *American Idol* past contestants, he made it all the way to the finale and became runner-up to the winner. Hundreds of thousands of fans looked on and were stunned that he didn't win. Nonetheless, he went on to become a world star and his dreams manifested way beyond his imagination. He is now playing to sold-out venues around the world and has a devoted fan following.

I share this example because I want to press the point to you that when things seem bleak and are not going your way, I encourage you to never give up. Never give up on your dreams, no matter how frustrated you may become. Keep your eye on the prize and stay focused on what you want. If you are reading this book right now, it is because I followed one of my dreams and never gave up.

I encourage you to search your heart and soul and realize your dreams. Don't limit yourself. Believe in yourself and believe you deserve your dream life. Remember, many of the limitations in your life are those you impose on yourself. If you doubt yourself, you will create situations to sabotage yourself and your dream. Only see your desired results. Focus on them whenever you can. Your thoughts are more powerful than you can imagine. As you focus on your dream life, you will feel happy and fulfilled. Your emotions will let you know if you are on the right path. Pay attention and follow the bread crumbs. Remember, the bread crumbs are circumstances that will show up in your life to guide you on your dream path. Never lose sight of your dream and never give up. Believe in yourself and that you deserve a happy, abundant life. That abundant life will find you. As you dream, relax and allow it to come to you. Stay in the flow, pay attention to the good things coming your way, and always remember to appreciate.

FOLLOWING YOUR PASSIONS

*When I follow my passions in life, I bring myself
and others around me happiness.*

*To be passionate is to be full of expression. To be able to
express this passion is exhilarating.*

A passion is something you love to do. When you are doing
or experiencing something you are passionate about,
you are excited, happy, and fulfilled. When you pursue

a passion, you feel alive. Without a passion you could become dull and stagnated. You may feel empty inside. We have learned about following your dreams and believing you deserve an abundant life. It is wonderful to dream, but without living or following your passions, you may be limiting yourself from the vibrant, creative person that you are. When we follow and act on our passions the world usually benefits. Passions are usually creative endeavors. Passions could be anything from the arts to athletic abilities to nature to entertainment or simply just relaxing and appreciating a good book or music. To discover your passion, think about what it is you do that really makes you happy. Acting on what we are passionate about can give us deep and lasting fulfillment. Often, sharing this passion with others can create happiness and excitement in their lives as well.

Being passionate about something can be infectious. Happiness and excitement are infectious. When others see this and feel this excitement from you, they want it, too. You may inspire others to find and follow their own passion, thus creating a little more happiness in this world. I encourage you to dream big and follow the bread crumbs to lead you towards that dream. I encourage you to follow your passions to create happiness and fulfillment in your and others' lives. As you are following your dreams and passions, remember that continuous appreciation will help keep your dreams and passions alive.

APPRECIATION

To appreciate is to give out love.

When I appreciate, I always feel happy.

When I appreciate all that I have today, I will have more to appreciate tomorrow.

When I give out love and appreciation, love and appreciation always find their way back to me.

True happiness starts with appreciation. If you don't have appreciation, then you have taken all of the good things around you for granted. You may only be noticing the negative. When you live with negative thoughts and mistrust of your surroundings, do you think this will bring you happiness and fulfillment? Do you think living in fear and mistrust will guide you towards your desired journey? I'm sure you would all agree with a no answer to these questions. To live with appreciation and thankfulness automatically gives you a happy, peaceful feeling deep within. You will find that the more you are thankful for and appreciate each day, the more you will have to be thankful for and appreciate in your tomorrows.

If you find yourself in a depressed state and wondering what you have to be thankful for, let me help you. I believe you can take a grain of sand and make mountains out of it. If you are feeling sad right now, for any number of reasons, let's start with just a grain of sand. I know that if you search, you will find something to be thankful for and be appreciative of in your everyday life. First let's start with your health. Is there something about your health to be thankful for? Are you able to see? Are you able to smell? Are you able to hear? Are you able to taste? Are you able to feel touch? Are you able to speak or communicate in some way? Are you able to move from point A to point B? Do you have food to eat? Do you have clean water to drink? Do you have shelter? Are you safe at night when you go to sleep? Do you have a blanket to keep you warm? Now let's look at friends and family. Are there those around you that love and support you? Is there someone you can reach out and touch or that reaches out to touch you? Can you see in the eyes of that someone that he/she cares about you?

If you answer yes to any of these questions, you then have your grain of sand. I would imagine that most of you reading this book can answer yes to most of these questions. If you have many yes answers then I must remind you that you are living in abundance and have much to be thankful for each day. So many times we take the little but most important things for granted. If one of these things is taken from us, we remember how important it was and may wish we had appreciated it more every day. Take a moment and think of all that you have in your life to be appreciative of. If you have friends and family in your life, let them know how much you appreciate them. It's also nice to let them know exactly what you appreciate them for. You will probably receive more of it from them. Appreciation leads to free happiness. It doesn't cost anything, and it can offer you and others much fulfillment.

When you go to sleep each evening with thankfulness in your heart, you go to sleep with peace. When you awake each morning with appreciation for all that you have, you start the day with a positive energy that will only bring more to be thankful for during the day. I'm sure we all know what it feels like to go to sleep focusing on what we don't have, feeling stress and disharmony. How do you sleep when you go to sleep worrying about something? How do you feel when you wake up? You will actually start the day with more of the same—stress, anxiety, mistrust, and disharmony. Your focus will continue to be on scarcity and fear, and you will continue to draw this into your life. I encourage you to appreciate each day, because you really do have so much if you take the time to notice it and pay attention.

I do understand that when you are in a depressed state, it can be hard to appreciate what you have. I have been there. Being sad may be comforting to you because it has become a habitual emotion and it is what you are used to. This is when I encourage and urge you to move out of this habitual sadness and mistrust. Take one thing to be thankful for each day and build on it. Focus on appreciating any one thing that you have been blessed with, and never allow your thoughts to go negative or think about what you lack or don't have. This is your grain of sand.

Maybe you can focus on the fact that you have food to eat. Maybe you can focus on the fact that you have shelter of some form. Maybe you could focus on the fact that you can speak, hear, taste, smell, and see. There are so many things to be thankful for. Take that grain of sand and build on it each day. From this you can build a castle. Focus on that one thing to be thankful for the whole day. Go to sleep being thankful for it. With each new day, add to your appreciation list. As the days go by, soon you will come to realize you may have everything you need. Hopefully your depression will lift and happiness will surround you. Take that grain of sand and create mountains of abundance in your life. You are surrounded with opportunities to have and become anything you desire. It is your life and your choice to appreciate. Just know that there are many in this world that would love to have the abundance you have but have found themselves in circumstances beyond their control. This is when we all should take notice of others that might need our help.

UNEXPLAINABLE TRUTHS

I understand that my neighbors in my community and across the globe have needs. I give back what I can. I am aware of their sufferings and I send them LOVE.

I may be a dreamer, but I hope someday you will join me and the world can live as one.

There are many disturbing situations in life and on this earth that I cannot explain. Many people have little opportunity to further their dreams simply because of the environment they live in. Their dreams may be simply to survive another day, or for their family or loved ones to survive another day. I cannot explain why there are so many without simple life necessities, such as clean drinking water, food, shelter, and a feeling of safety at night as they sleep. My heart breaks for so many who have fallen victim to crimes against them. I can never explain nor try to understand small children being kidnapped for the perpetrator's sexual pleasure and then being tossed away or discarded. I can never explain the torture or infliction of pain on anyone. So many innocent people have found themselves in harm's way in the midst of a war fueled by greed, power, lust, and, yes, religion. I cannot explain these crimes against humanity; however, I feel it is important to include information about these unexplainable truths in this book, written from my heart, about self-empowerment and teachings of how to create true peace and happiness in one's life. I titled this chapter "Unexplainable Truths" because, though I teach about self-empowerment, unfortunately there are some situations involving innocent victims that may feel powerless due to their life circumstances. How do you empower someone who is a victim of someone or something larger than themselves? I have offered self-love as a universal answer and I believe in it strongly, but I feel compelled to share some unexplainable truths in an effort to reach out to those still in need of help. Most who offered critique of my book urged me to remove this chapter, as they did not see its relevance in the overall theme of my writing. I am compelled to include it, though, to offer a voice for those who are unable to speak of their injustice. Please read in the context of my intention.

What I am about to write, many may not want to hear. Most of us are drawn towards light, happiness, fun, and the easy road. Most don't want to read or hear about the sufferings of others. We may get so caught up in our daily lives and routines, along with our own created worries that we don't want to turn our attention to that which may cause us to cringe or feel upset inside. Yes, I understand this, as I have just spent many pages urging you to focus only on positive and happy thoughts. The fact is, though, that there are many that share our planet with us who are suffering. It is important for us to become aware of the inhumanity that exists around us so those of us who are living in comfort can reach out and help those less fortunate. If reading about inhumane acts makes you uncomfortable then please skip to the following chapter, "Giving Back". I understand that it is sometimes hard to comprehend heinous acts upon fellow humans, and even innocent children. I am compelled to be their voice though, encouraging all that can, to lend a hand and stop the suffering. If you choose to continue through this chapter, the following are examples of my unexplainable truths.

From the beginning of time, man has waged war against his fellow humans for nothing more than greed, the need for more land and/or power, and against ideological differences. Many times war and killings take place because one group of people wants to overpower another group of people who may be disadvantaged due to race, stature, gender, or religious beliefs. Many have been taken as slaves to serve a more powerful group. The slave then becomes the other person's property and is expected to perform at the command of his/her master. Where is the love for humanity in this act of hurting another for one's own pleasure or selfishness? In slavery, the master removes all human rights from the enslaved person and has the slave do acts against his/her will. This is exploitation of power toward another living person. Slavery continues to this day in many parts of the world, as is seen in human trafficking. Women and children are often the victims in this despicable act, and most of it revolves around making them sex slaves for the pleasure of another. Drugs play an important role in keeping the victims subdued.

We all recall the genocide that took place in World War II when Hitler's army attempted to exterminate the Jewish race from the earth. The Nazis executed twelve million civilians, six million of whom were Jews. In total, fifty million people lost their lives in this war. Five thousand Jewish communities were wiped out. A third of the Jewish population was exterminated. When this war ended, the Jews that were imprisoned in the concentration camps were freed. Many were on the verge of starvation and had lived through events that most of us could never even fathom. Many survived on hope alone. Most of the world was astonished by this atrocity and agreed that never again would this be allowed to happen. Unfortunately, genocide continues to take place today, and the world looks on.

In 1994 the Rwanda genocide took place. Starting April 6, 1994, there were one hundred days of mass murder by the Hutu tribe in an attempt to exterminate the Tutsi people. In just one hundred days, eight hundred thousand Tutsis were killed by the Hutu militia using clubs and machetes. Neighbors were forced to kill other neighbors. Even spouses were forced to kill their Tutsi spouses. No one was spared. Men, women, children, and babies were killed. There were close to ten thousand Tutsis killed each day. This atrocity ended after Tutsi rebels from neighboring countries managed to defeat the Hutus and stop the genocide in July 1994. Today, healing and forgiveness have replaced the hatred and senseless killings amongst the Rwandans. There is now reconciliation and unity amongst both tribes.

This information may be gut-wrenching to hear and read about, but I must go on in an effort to increase our awareness in hope that many will reach out in some way to help relieve others suffering and stop this madness. When we give out to those in need, goodness always finds its way back to us. Our planet is full of those living with scarcity and with the lack of life's simple necessities for a healthy survival. There are also many innocents found in harm's way of someone else's war. Some are even abducted into the war against their will. Their safety is also a concern.

Many of our fellow humans' needs are plentiful, but my personal passions have led me to the sufferings of those in the African countries. Today the many corrupt leaders of these countries continue to deny so many innocent people the rights to survive with dignity and peace. Their people have suffered and continue to struggle for survival. While I focus my attention on the plight of those in the African countries, I do not belittle the struggle of those in less-fortunate areas around the world, including the USA and European nations that need help with food, shelter, and health care.

There is a genocide currently taking place in the African country of Sudan. The Sudanese government has ordered the Sudanese security forces and the Janjaweed (Arab militias) to systematically destroy the indigenous Sudanese people by bombing and burning villages, looting economic resources, and murdering, raping, and torturing noncombatant civilians. More than three hundred thousand civilians have died due to violence, malnutrition, and disease. Over 2.7 million people have been displaced within Sudan and have taken up refuge in the camps of Darfur. An additional 250,000 have crossed over the border into the neighboring country of Chad to take refuge in similar camps. These camps have little food, water, and health care. Direct violence continues today as I write. In March 2009 the International Criminal Court issued an arrest warrant for the president of Sudan, Omar al-Bashir, for crimes against humanity. Because of this, his retaliation was to order eighteen humanitarian agencies to leave his country, leaving millions of refugees without food, drinking water, and medical aide. As a consequence, millions of the Sudanese refugees' lives are at risk.

In neighboring countries, war in the Democratic Repub-
lic of Congo (DRC) has ravaged the country since 1989.
Since then, 5.4 million people have died, as many as forty-
five thousand each month, according to the International
Rescue Committee. It has become one of the world's dead-
liest documented conflicts since World War II. Many rebel
groups have risen up and are fighting each other, as well
as the Congolese army, for access and control of eastern
Congo's mineral reserve. Many also die from preventable
diseases such as malaria, diarrhea, pneumonia, and malnutrition, as well as lack of nutritious food, sanitation, and
access to basic health care. Children bear the brunt of this
health crisis, contributing to half of the deaths.

In Uganda there have been more than two decades
of fighting between the LRA (Lord's Resistance Army) and
the Ugandan military. A total of 1.8 million people were displaced and many killed. The fighting has now subsided in
many areas of the country and some are starting to return
home, but many still don't have safe water, health care, or
education services in their areas.

Joseph Kony is the notorious leader of the LRA and is well
known for abducting children and making them fight as soldiers. The LRA has abducted more than thirty thousand child
soldiers and slaves in its twenty-year war against the Ugandan government. Once captured, the young boys and girls
are given drugs and forced to watch violent movies over
and over again at night to desensitize them. If they tried
to escape and were caught, they were tortured, killed, or
mutilated, many times by fellow child soldiers. These children were forced to loot, burn villages, rape, torture, and
kill neighbors. The girls that were abducted were routinely
raped and became sex slaves to the rebel commanders.
Many did not survive. If the parents tried to stop the abduction of their children, they were killed. The conflict in northern
Uganda has forced tens of thousands of children to travel

to town centers at night to avoid violence and abduction. This abduction of children for the purpose of making them soldiers continues today.

In conflict areas, violence against women and young girls has become a constant. During war times they are subjected to rape, violent physical assault, abduction into sexual slavery, are forcibly married and impregnated, and are forced to trade sex for survival. In many of the African countries where civil war has been or is taking place, there is unimaginable brutality against women and young girls. Many are brutally gang raped to a point of causing severe medical damage and even death. The raping is another weapon aimed at complete physical and psychological destruction of the women to destroy their entire society. They are often shamed, socially stigmatized, and denied compensation. Rape has become another form of genocide.

Today rape continues to be a problem in many African countries. A hospital in the DRC has the sole purpose of caring for women who are rape victims. They are currently receiving at least thirty women a month who are the victims of gang rapes, beatings, stabbings, and sexual violation. Often husbands, fathers, and sons are being beaten, forced to watch or play dead nearby.

When will the world take notice and put a stop to these atrocities? When will the world start paying attention?

Southern Africa has experienced a starvation and famine crisis due to drought conditions. There are seventy-five thousand children under the age of five who need therapeutic and supplementary nutrition support today. Some 4.5 million Ethiopians are in need of emergency food. There is a lack of safe drinking water in many of the regions and insufficient medical care.

Africa also has the world's biggest HIV crisis. AIDS has infected 60 percent of its population. It was estimated that twenty-two million people were infected with HIV at the end of 2007. In 2008, 1.5 million died from AIDS and more than eleven million children were orphaned. Young children without wage-earning potential are left to care for themselves and their younger siblings. Their childhood has been snatched from them and they are forced into adult responsibilities with only child capabilities. Help must be sent their way because their young little lives deserve better.

All of these unexplainable truths are staggering and tug at one's heart. Most of them are preventable, and many of them are crimes committed by one human to another. Indigenous people throughout the centuries, such as the Native American Indians, Amazonian Indians, Aboriginals, and South Pacific Islanders, have been killed or displaced due to another's desire to overtake their land. During the days when Rome was flourishing, the Roman Coliseum was a place where crowds gathered to witness the killings and suffering of others. They cheered over fights to the death between wild animals, animals vs. people, and gladiators against each other. The games in Rome are known today as the bloodiest exhibitions of public entertainment known to mankind. When will these senseless crimes against others on our planet end? Can we stop it? I do believe that if we all did our part, each of us picking an area of need and giving to it in some way, we could make a difference to end some of the suffering and make this world a better, happier place for all those that inhabit it.

John Lennon wrote the song "Imagine." I will summarize his words, as I find them very appropriate to bring us back together from the above-written atrocities:

Imagine that we had no heaven and no hell, only sky above.

I may be a dreamer, but I hope someday you will join me and the world can live as one.

Imagine that we had no countries and no religion, too. Imagine all of the people living as one.

I may be a dreamer, but I hope someday you will join me and the world can live as one.

Imagine there is nothing to kill or die for, and no religion, too. Imagine if all of the people were living a life for peace.

I may be a dreamer, but I hope someday you will join me and the world can live as one.

Imagine no possessions and no need for greed or hunger. Just a brotherhood of man, sharing all the world.

I may be a dreamer, but I hope someday you will join me and the world can live as one.

GIVING BACK

When I give back to the world, the world responds with healing to those who are suffering.

When I give, I feel a sense of warmth, peace, and love.

Giving is always a feeling of receiving more than I have to give.

I am thankful for all that I have, and I pass it on.

If each person on this planet did one thing to help his/her brothers and sisters around the world, we could make a difference to end the pain and suffering of those less fortunate. Many of us live in comfort and are only afflicted by our own psychological demons. I have described how to rid those negative thoughts from your head and create better choices that draw in more comfort and peace. Through believing in the positive and appreciating all that we have, we can live our individual lives with more peace and harmony. When we live with more peace and happiness, we are then able to pass it on to make this world a better place. You have also learned how to find deep love for yourself. By attaching your heart to all that is good in this world, you can have continuous peace and trust. We can then pass this on to create more peace around us.

To give is to receive, and to receive is to give. It is a circle. There are so many ways to give back to the world. For your convenience, I have added an appendix at the end of this book with many website suggestions you can choose from, if you want to use this way to give back. We are all individuals and you will all have your own preferences as to where and how you want to give. As you give to the world, the world will give back to you, and you will continue the circle. It will continue to create abundance in your life as you pass this abundance on to others. Appreciate and teach those around you to appreciate. Each of us has so much to be thankful for, but there are those that have less and continue to have a daily struggle for survival. When you give back, you can give in your own neighborhood or you can give globally. As you become open to giving, you will see many needs around you. You will be drawn to that which is right for you. Follow your heart and passions, and pay attention to the bread crumbs that light up your path.

Reach your hand out. Touch your neighbor in your own community or your neighbor across the globe. We are all inter-connected, thus we must treat each other with respect and dignity. The Golden Rule, "Treat others as you would have others treat you," seems so simple, but the words, if carried out, are very powerful. Our current president of the United States, President Obama, has encouraged us all to give back in some way. We all know that most of us have at least one grain of sand to appreciate each day. Take that grain of sand of appreciation and pass it on. Sprinkle more love on your neighbors. When you give love and hope away each day, love and hope will always find their way back to you. It is the boomerang effect that I have taught my children from a young age. They learned early on that what they put out in this world, be it positive or negative, will always return to them. As you reach out to touch the life of another, you will reap fulfillment in many forms. Pay attention to what you give out. Believe in hope and pass it on. It is Their Life and Our Choice.

FINDING HOPE IN HOPELESSNESS

I am always able to find hope.

Hope brings me freedom and gives me life.

To hope is to live my life with a happy heart.

I am able to pass HOPE on to those in need.

Hope is free. Hope gives you a reason to go on. To hope is to believe that all is good and that every step you take will be for your own best interest. To hope is to trust. Hope will bring a smile to your face, a child's face, an elderly person's face, and your neighbor's face in the midst of tears. When you feel that all is hopeless, hope will take you through another day, believing that tomorrow the sun will rise again. Hope is knowing you deserve better. With each ending, hope knows there will be a new beginning. As the sun sets, hope assures you that the beauty of a new sunrise will be upon you. In suffering, the touch of another will bring hope. A gentle touch, a loving look, brings hope back into your heart. A rainbow follows every storm to remind you hope is still alive and thriving. A stranger's eyes offer hope as they send you a caring gaze. Babies feel hope in the arms of someone sending them love and safety. Hope in each of us builds as our trust in others becomes renewed from their love and giving. Giving is receiving, and hope is a gift each of us has to give.

Hope is free to each of us. Hope will keep your dreams alive. Hope will guide you home. Hope will guide you to your inner being, where love abounds in an endless source. Hope is available for all who seek it. Let's pass it on.

Your Life, Your Choice: Overview

I have made the point over and over again that your life **is** your choice. We have learned that everything we have in our life is because of our choices, thoughts, and actions. If there is something in our life we would like to change, we have learned that we alone have the power within us to be and do anything we set our mind to. We are our only limitations. We have learned that when we maintain an Open Heart, love and light are able to thrive and grow in each of us. That light shines on our path, leading us home and back to the beginning of where we started when we came into this world, back to our own spirit of eternal love.

As we review, it is good to remember that light and love in our lives guide us to our inner peace and harmony. They remind us who we really are and of are our own personal connections with our Spirit. Through our connection to our inner spirit, we can find our own self-worth and self-love. With this we learn to stand firm and become our own beautiful tree, standing strong with deep, growing roots. Our leaves are bright and beautiful, and as we shine, we offer love out to others.

We have learned that by paying attention to our emotions and how we are feeling, we can make healthier choices in our lives. We now understand that when we are feeling excited or exhilarated about a choice that we have made, we are on the right path to fulfilling our dreams. We also understand that when we feel tense, anxious, and have trouble sleeping while we worry about a choice, we may have made a wrong turn away from our path towards abundance in our lives. As we turn and go into a different direction and start to feel happy, light, and excited again, we can be assured we have put ourselves back on course.

We have also learned to take responsibility for our lives, as we now understand that it is only we who have chosen how we acted or reacted in certain situations. Actions or nonactions have all been our choices and have created the circumstances we currently have in our lives today. It is our responsibility to change our current life circumstances if we are unhappy with them or change the way we think about them. There is always a positive view in each situation, and when we focus on the positive, the situation will soon become something that will cause us more happiness.

When we find ourselves at an ending, or at a completion of a certain chapter or stage in our life, it is important to take a time-out that allows us time to heal and grieve. Engaging back into life too quickly after suffering a loss may lead to a prolonged grieving cycle. The pain of our loss will continue unless we allow ourselves time to heal and come out the other side, with a renewed desire to engage in life again. As we have nurtured ourselves sufficiently, we can then begin a healthy transition back into our normal life endeavors. Because we have taken time to heal, our future interactions will come from a strong and healthy foundation full of self-love.

Relationships are important in one's life, as they give us a way to give and receive love. If we are able to truly appreciate and love ourselves, we are able to give and receive love in a balanced, harmonious way with another. This balance of appreciating, giving, and receiving provides a healthy foundation for any relationship. Once you have obtained this relationship balance, appreciate it every day, because you have truly been blessed.

Fear is in opposition to love. To worry is to give in to fear. Fear has no place in a healthy, balanced individual. Fear comes from mistrust and produces defenses in an individual to prevent others from coming to close. When we open to love and realize we carry the love from our inner spirit with us wherever we go, we no longer have to live in fear. Love dissipates fear. Love also produces forgiveness for those who you may feel have harmed you in your past. Pure forgiveness and love lead to trust. Trust makes you feel safe. Trust gives you peace in believing that all that happens to you will lead you on your journey towards your abundance. Abundance comes from appreciating. The more you appreciate, the more abundance you will have in your life to appreciate.

We have also learned that we have created all that we see when we look in the mirror. By leading a life with more emphasis on health and fitness, we know our self-image will improve. As we learn that we have control of what we put into and outside of our bodies, we have learned to make better choices in creating balance within our bodies. We have learned that it is our body and our choice to treat it kindly. We are all created beautiful, and it is our choice to continue nurturing our inner beauty, which leads to outer beauty.

We know that by changing our habitual patterns with healthy actions, we can lead a happier, more harmonious life. We can change our patterns by changing our story. As we dream, we should dream big and know that we can accomplish anything we desire if we continually focus our thoughts and positive feelings in this direction. When we change our thoughts to what we want our lives to look like, our actions and choices will reflect that which we desire. I encourage you all to dream big. Reflect on your dream life often and never give up. Soon your dream life will become your reality. Your dreams are free for all of you to partake in. Dream it, feel it, and then allow it to show up in your life. When you see the bread crumbs leading you to your dream life, acknowledge and appreciate them, encouraging them to come more often, leading you to your heart's desires.

There are many unexplainable truths in this world which have caused much unnecessary suffering amongst our global brothers and sisters. Unexplainable atrocities have been happening to mankind since the beginning of time. Many are from humans harming other humans due to greed, lust or desire for more power. A solution in stopping or curbing this madness is for all of us to give back to those less fortunate. In doing this, we are creating more love and peace in this world. If each of us picked one area of suffering and offered some form of hope in that direction, this world would become of a planet filled with more peace and harmony for all whom exist here. I share in John Lennon's dream as he expressed it in his song "Imagine" that we can all live as one. We share this planet with our brothers and sisters. Our planet needs to be treated with love and kindness as we care for ourselves and for our neighbors. As we pass love on, love will always find its way back to us.

There is always hope. Hope is the light in every darkness. Each of you now have the tools to take that grain of sand and create hope, appreciation, and abundance in your life. You understand that in sharing love with others, you are in turn receiving. As you pass this on, we can now create love, peace, and harmony within us and all around us.

Thank you for opening your heart and sharing this journey with me from darkness into light. May light and love abound in all of you as you now know how to create and journey into a life filled with peace, harmony, and balance yourselves. As you pass this on, may it multiply throughout our world in abundance. It is Our Life, Our World, and Our Choice.

I hope you have enjoyed the gift I have given to you through this book, *Open Heart, Your Life Your Choice*, as it flowed from my open heart to yours. May the words guide you and remind you, as you continue on your journey through life, that love, comfort, true happiness, and inner harmony are there for all that seek it. May your heart stay open, because it is **Your Life** and **Your Choice.**

I understand that My Life is My Choice,
and I now choose wisely.

I am able to create my life through a complete
integration of a whole and healthy being
spiritually, emotionally, and physically.

It is my life, and I choose peace, harmony, and happiness.

I choose Self-love, and I choose to pass Love on.

AFFIRMATIONS

My Story

Sometimes, in order to find yourself, you must first lose yourself.

Light

Light is Love, and love is my connection to my Inner Spirit.
When I move towards the light, I find my peace.
When I gaze at the light, I feel a sense of warmth and protection.

Connection to Spirit

When I connect to my inner spirit, I feel peace, love, and joy.
When I connect to my inner spirit, I find balance and direction.
When I connect to my inner spirit, I find unconditional love.

Choices

I now make choices that are in perfect alignment with my soul desire and purpose, bringing more peace and harmony into my life.

Power of Thoughts

My thoughts are always positive, bringing more peace, harmony, and abundance into my life.
I focus my thoughts on appreciation and my life's desires.
I understand that my thoughts create my future, so I only focus on what I want my life to look like.
I am thankful for all that I have.
I am the creator of my reality through my thoughts.

Taking Responsibility
I take full responsibility for my life and how I have created it.
I forgive myself and others from my past.
I have the power to create my life just the way I want it.

Standing at the Crossroads
I have positive thoughts when I go to sleep and when I awake.
Positive thoughts today bring about a more positive tomorrow.
I live a live full of balance, peace, and harmony.

Letting Go
I have let go of the past and allow all that is good to come to me now.
I trust that all that comes to me is for my best interest when I visualize my desires and let go of attachments.

Stages of Grief
I have allowed myself to go through the stages of grief in a healthy manner, and I am now free to experience my new and exciting life as a whole and healthy being.

Single and Dating
I am a whole and healthy being and therefore attract only whole and healthy beings into my life.
I only allow loving and caring beings into my inner circle.
I have attracted the perfect partner and now have a loving, harmonious relationship full of understanding and balance.

Relationships
I have a wonderful, stable, harmonious relationship full of love, caring, giving, and understanding.
My partner and I are each other's best friends and lovers.

I have an equal balance of giving and receiving in my partnership, and we are very happy together.

In my relationship there is trust, respect, stability, and harmony.

My partner and I appreciate each other daily.

Cheating, Lies, and Affairs

I understand that it is in my best interest to feed and cultivate the relationship I am currently in.

I choose to be the best partner I can in my current relationship.

I choose to look for positive attributes in my current partner and remember why I was attracted to him/her in the beginning.

I act with integrity and dignity in all areas of my life.

I am honest with myself and love myself; therefore, I only allow myself to be in healthy relationships with those that treat me with love and respect.

Addictions

I now have the power to be free and love myself.

I make only healthy choices for my life.

I am a whole, healthy being in every area of my life.

I live a life of balance.

I have courage and strength to only seek for myself all that is good and all that is positive.

Being in Balance

I live a life full of balance and wellness.

I create a balanced life of work, play, rest, and rejuvenation.

Because I live in balance, I live in harmony.

Self-love

I love myself and only allow situations and people into my life that reflect this back to me.

When I love myself, I am able to give and receive love freely.

Fear vs. Love
I choose to live my life full of love.
I give and receive love easily.
Love surrounds my life in every way.

Anger
I always choose understanding, love, and kindness.
I take a time-out when needed and always return to love.

Forgiveness
I am easily able to forgive and offer love.
I forgive myself and others from any past hurts.
I now have freedom in forgiveness.

Trust
I live with trust that everything that comes to me is in my best interest.
When I trust, I feel free and live in peace.

Parenting
As a parent, I create an environment of safety and trust for my children.
I guide my children through life but also allow them enough autonomy to evolve into healthy, responsible adults.
I instill self-confidence and self-love in my children by always making them feel loved and supported.

Self-image
I love myself and understand that I have created everything I see when I look in the mirror.
When I look in the mirror, I am pleased with what I see.
I love myself inside and out and make healthy choices that mirror this love back to me.

Eating Habits

I eat foods that my body needs for fuel and am able to balance the caloric intake for my body to be healthy and strong.

I eat fun foods in small quantities, with a healthy balance of good foods.

I eat until I'm full and then stop, understanding my body's needs.

I eat plenty of foods that are healthy for me, such as fresh fruits, vegetables, and lean protein.

I have healthy eating habits.

Health and Fitness

My body is healthy and strong, and I incorporate a regular exercise program into my life.

I am able to create myself as a whole and healthy being, physically, emotionally, and spiritually.

I eat foods that are healthy and good for me.

I love myself as a healthy and fit being.

Repeating Patterns

In my life I am able to learn from my past and now make healthy choices.

I have a life full of balance, peace, and harmony.

I only attract that which is healthy and positive to me.

I am a whole, healthy individual and live a life full of abundance.

Change Your Story

I now tell a story of abundance and have abundance in my life in every way.

My story now reflects one of health and fitness, and my life has responded with a healthy and fit body.

My story now tells of having loving, harmonious relationships in my life, and my life reflects this back to me.

Having a Dream
As I dream and envision what I want my reality to be, my future reality becomes my dream.
When I envision my dream life, I feel happy and elated.
As I dream, I am creating my future.
When I dream, I dream big, because I realize I can be and do anything I dream of.

Follow Your Passions
When I follow my passions in life, I bring myself and others around me happiness.
To be passionate is to be full of expression. To be able to express this passion is exhilarating.

Appreciation
To appreciate is to give out love.
When I appreciate, I always feel happy.
When I appreciate all that I have today, I will have more to appreciate tomorrow.
When I give out love and appreciation, love and appreciation always finds their way back to me.

Unexplainable Truths
I understand that my neighbors in my community and across the globe have needs. I give back what I can. I am aware of their sufferings and I send them LOVE.
I may be a dreamer, but I hope someday you will join me and the world can live as one.

Giving Back
When I give back to the world, the world responds with healing to those who are suffering
When I give, I feel a sense of warmth, peace, and love
Giving is always a feeling of receiving more than I have to give.
I am thankful for all that I have, and I pass it on.

Hope

I am always able to find hope.
Hope brings me freedom and gives me life.
To hope is to live my life with a happy heart.
I am able to pass HOPE on to those in need.

Your Life, Your Choice

I understand that My Life is My Choice, and I now choose wisely.
I am able to create my life through a complete integration of a whole and healthy being spiritually, emotionally and physically.
It is my life, and I choose peace, harmony, and happiness.
I choose Self-Love, and I choose to pass Love on.

Appendix A
HOW CAN I HELP?
GIVING BACK

"Give to the world your best
And the best will return to you"

The following websites are only suggestions for giving back. Being unique individuals, we are each passionate about different areas needing assistance, therefore choosing our own specific ways to give back to this world. I respect and encourage this in all forms. Please note that many of the websites below are African genocide sites. Much of my passion is directed in this area due to the fact that atrocities continue to take place in the country of Sudan, the Congo, and neighboring African countries.

On another note, the sites below to sponsor a child are ones that I currently use. I have been very happy with them and receive correspondence and updated pictures from my children regularly.

To Sponsor a Child:
www.planusa.org

Plan USA - Plan is an international children's development agency with no religious or political affiliation. It works in about 50 developing countries around the world, aiming to overcome poverty and secure a brighter future for children and their families worldwide. Your sponsorship links you with a child and family in a poor country — while your ongoing sponsorship contributions make possible life-changing pro-grams in health care, education and a better quality of life for children, their families and communities. In addition to building schools, health clinics, latrines, and clean-water wells, the ongoing commitment of child sponsorship allows a steady stream of funds that Plan can effectively allocate to ensure community development and help break the painful cycle of poverty for millions of children and their families.

www.worldvision.com

World Vision is a Christian relief, development and advo-cacy organization dedicated to working with children, families and communities to overcome poverty and injus-tice. Because poverty has both local and global causes, World Vision works within communities and across geo-graphical areas to help individuals and groups improve the well-being of children and overcome poverty. You can personally reach out and connect with a child and community. You get to see and feel the difference your support makes, through the eyes of your sponsored child and their letters and photographs. Sponsorship provides resources that go into programs that are usually ten to fifteen years in length and are custom-designed in collaboration with community leaders to address key needs. Programs are child-focused but also benefit non-sponsored children and families.

- This sponsorship provides the best communication with my child in receiving updated pictures and letters.

Be the Change, Save a Life site:
www.saveone.net

Be the Change: Save a Life is a global health initiative presented by ABC News to bring attention to today's most pressing health challenges, and to inspire people to act.

ABC News is launching a year-long project to focus attention on the diseases and health conditions that disproportionately impact the world's poorest people. Here you'll find the latest news on today's most pressing global health concerns: from malaria and HIV/AIDS, to maternal and child health, to neglected tropical diseases, and more.

Two global health concerns that stand out for me on this site, and that I currently support, are the topics of malnutrition and water and sanitation needs.

Malnutrition - nearly 150 million children under five are malnourished, and malnutrition is the underlying cause of most childhood illness and death. In the last two years, the cases of malnutrition are higher than they've been in that last century. Malnutrition affects an estimated two billion people and kills more than 3.5 million children under five years old each year.

Plumpy'nut, a peanut paste packed with calories and nutrients, has been found to be one of the most effective ways to treat malnutrition and can transform a child's health in a matter of weeks. A small donation monthly provides one child one month of treatment.

Water and Sanitation - Almost a billion people on the planet don't have access to clean, safe drinking water. Unsafe water and lack of basic sanitation cause 80% of diseases and kill more people every year than all forms of violence, including war. In Ethiopia alone, 83 million people lack access to safe water sources. Many live in rural areas and must walk miles each day to collect water that's likely to make them sick. Waterborne disease is one of the leading causes of death to kids under five years old in Ethiopia.

A small donation here can buy 2,000 chlorine tablets to treat dirty water. **UNICEF** delivers the chlorine tablets to families who need them in the developing world, giving them access to safe drinking water. ***Charity*** is another organization committed to providing safe and clean drinking water to developing countries. 100% of donations received by *charity: water* directly fund sustainable water projects in areas of greatest need.

Overall, this website provides many opportunities to get involved and give back to those in need with life threatening health challenges. Besides malnutrition and safe drinking water, many health issues are covered such as sponsoring safe birthing kits, baby warmers, HIV/TB treatment, and getting medicine to remote communities.

Stop Genocide and Action Sites:
www.physiciansforhumanrights.org
Physicians for Human Rights mobilizes health professionals to advance health, dignity and justice, and promotes the right to health for all. Harnessing the specialized skills, rigor, and passion of doctors, nurses, public health specialists and scientists, PHR investigates human rights abuses and works to stop them.

Their research takes them to conflict zones, to AIDS-ravaged Africa, to US prisons and immigration detention centers — and their advocacy brings them to the offices of national and international policymakers. The courts, decision makers and the media have come to rely on their credibility and expertise. Motivated by moral urgency, based on science, and anchored in international human rights standards, PHR's advocacy advances global health and protects human rights.

www.savedarfur.org

Savedarfur is an agency which stands together to unite voices to raise public awareness and mobilize a massive response to the atrocities in Sudan's western region of Darfur.

Responding to a rebellion in 2003, the regime of Sudanese President Omar al-Bashir and its allied militia, known as the *Janjaweed,* launched a campaign of destruction against the civilian population of ethnic groups identified with the rebels. They wiped out entire villages, destroyed food and water supplies, stole livestock and systematically murdered, tortured and raped civilians. The Sudanese government's genocidal, scorched earth campaign has claimed hundreds of thousands of lives through direct violence, disease and starvation, and continues to destabilize the region. Millions have fled their homes and live in dangerous camps in Darfur, and hundreds of thousands are refugees in neighboring Chad. Violence continues today. Ultimately, the fate of the Darfuri people depends on establishing a lasting and just peace in all of Sudan and in the region.

This agency is committed to the goals that the Save Darfur Coalition advocates for, including:
- Ending the violence against civilians;
- Facilitating adequate and unhindered humanitarian aid;

- Establishing conditions for the safe and voluntary return of displaced people to their homes;
- Promoting the long-term sustainable development of Darfur; and
- Holding the perpetrators accountable

They call on the United States, other governments, the United Nations and regional organizations to focus their efforts on ending this crisis.

www.theirc.org

The International Rescue Committee responds to the world's worst humanitarian crises and helps people to survive and rebuild their lives. Founded in 1933 at the request of Albert Einstein, the IRC offers lifesaving care and life-changing assistance to refugees forced to flee from war or disaster. At work today in over 40 countries and in 22 U.S. cities, the IRC restores safety, dignity and hope to millions who are uprooted and struggling to endure. The IRC leads the way from harm to home. When an emergency arises, the IRC arrives on the scene within 72 hours with urgently needed supplies and expertise that protect people caught in the midst of chaos. They commit to **stay as long as we are needed,** helping survivors to heal, recover and rebuild their communities to be stronger, more stable and more democratic. In the United States, the IRC has helped hundreds of thousands of refugees **thrive in the country that gave them sanctuary** and a new beginning.

www.ajws.org

American Jewish World Service (AJWS) is an international development organization motivated by Judaism's imperative to pursue justice. AJWS is dedicated to alleviating poverty, hunger and disease among the people of the developing world regardless of race, religion or nationality.

218

Through grants to grassroots organizations, volunteer service, advocacy and education, AJWS fosters civil society, sustainable development and human rights for all people, while promoting the values and responsibilities of global citizenship within the Jewish community.

www.jewishworldwatch.org

Jewish World Watch (JWW) is a hands-on leader in the fight against genocide and mass atrocities, engaging individuals and communities to take local actions that produce powerful global results. Founded in 2004 by Rabbi Harold M. Schulweis and Janice Kamenir-Reznik as the Jewish response to the genocide in Darfur, it has grown from a collection of Southern California synagogues into a global coalition that includes schools, churches, individuals, communities and partner organizations that share a vision of a world without genocide. JWW bears witness to firsthand accounts in conflict regions, partners with on-the-ground organizations to develop high-impact projects that improve the lives of survivors and help build the foundation for a safer world, and inspires our communities to support tangible projects and advocate for political change. JWW has raised more than five million dollars for relief and development projects that impact tens of thousands of people in Sudan and Congo.

www.invisiblechildren.com

In the spring of 2003, three young filmmakers traveled to Africa in search of a story. What started out as a filmmaking adventure transformed into much more when these boys from Southern California discovered a tragedy that disgusted and inspired them, a tragedy where children are both the weapons and the victims.

After returning to the States, they created the documentary "Invisible Children: Rough Cut," a film that exposes the tragic realities of northern Uganda's night commuters and child soldiers.

The film was originally shown to friends and family, but has now been seen by millions of people. The overwhelming response has been, "How can I help?" To answer this question, the non-profit Invisible Children, Inc. was created, giving compassionate individuals an effective way to respond to the situation.

Invisible Children is a movement seeking to end the conflict in Uganda and stop the abduction of children for use as child soldiers.

Stoves for Darfur:
www.darfurstoves.org
The Darfur Stoves Project seeks to protect Darfuri women by providing them with specially developed stoves which require less firewood, hence decreasing women's exposure to violence while collecting firewood and their need to trade food rations for fuel. Their mission is to improve the safety and wellbeing of internally displaced persons in Darfur by providing fuel-efficient cookstoves. The Berkeley-Darfur Stove® requires less than half the fuel of traditional three stone fires, thus reducing the time women spend outside the safety of the camps collecting firewood while also decreasing their use of money and food rations to obtain fuel.

Baskets for Rwanda:
www.rwandabaskets.com
www.macys.com – Rwanda baskets
These Web sites pay the women from Rwanda who make these baskets. It gives them much-needed money to help feed, clothe, and provide medical care and school supplies for their families. The baskets are woven both by victims of genocide and the reconciled perpetrators them-

selves. In purchasing these baskets, you help provide hope for rebuilding Rwanda.

- I have purchased baskets from both of these sites and love them both. They make great gifts while giving back to those in need.

GIVE TO THE WORLD YOUR BEST AND THE BEST WILL RETURN TO YOU

ABOUT THE AUTHOR

"I wanted to be able to touch the lives of many and offer guidance to help make others' lives a little easier. I wrote this book through love and inspiration to offer those who seek it a pathway toward their own open heart."

Jan Campbell is an open heart surgical nurse and an ACE (American Council on Exercise) Certified Personal Trainer. She received a bachelor's degree in sociology/psychology from the University of California, San Diego, and a bachelor's of science degree in nursing from Sonoma State University. Campbell has been in private practice as a certified hypnotherapist. Campbell is a Life Choice Guide and now offers private sessions in guided visualization to help others realize their dreams. Lectures and seminars are also available on the many topics included in her book.

www.yourlifeyourchoice.net

yourlifeyourchoice@att.net